Mady Musiol • Magaly Villarroel

Merry Team

Teacher's Guide

1

Contents

Merry Team - Teacher's Guide 1
By Mady Musiol and Magaly Villarroel
Tel. +39 071 750 701 - Fax +39 071 977 851
e-mail: info@elionline.com

© 2007 ELI srl
PO Box 6 - 62019 Recanati - Italy

Eli Editorial Department: Beatrice Loreti, Marco Mercatali
Design: Studio Di Vita
Illustrations: Studio Di Vita
Cover Design: Studio Cornell sas
Cover illustration: C. Virgil

Printed in Italy - Grafiche Flaminia - Trevi (PG) 07.83.215.0

ISBN	978-88-536-1094-2	Pupil's Book 1
ISBN	978-88-536-1106-2	Teacher's Guide 1
ISBN	978-88-536-1100-0	Activity Book 1
ISBN	978-88-536-1109-3	Flashcards 1

Table of contents

Unit 0 - Hello!

Objectives: To introduce simple greetings. To present the characters.

Vocabulary: Rocky, Freddy, Suzy, red, yellow, blue, green.

Language: Hello! Hello my friends. I'm (Rocky). This is (Suzy). Point to Suzy. Listen and point. Colour (Rocky). Show me (red). Touch (blue).

Pronunciation: Pronouncing the unit vocabulary. Practising rhythm and intonation through a chant.

Strategies: Using a colour code to identify the characters. Associating spoken and written words with illustrations.

Unit 1 - My room

Objectives: To identify items of furniture and classroom objects. To count to three. To learn some classroom instructions. To complete assessment and self-assessment activities.

Vocabulary: room, table, chair, window, door, bed, pencil, book, rubber, one, two, three, yes, no, please, thank you.

Language: This is my (table). Is it a (table)? They are my friends. Pick up the (pencil). Pick it up, put it down. This is my room! I've got a table and two chairs. And look, this is my bed!

Pronunciation: Pronouncing the unit vocabulary. Using the correct intonation in yes/no questions. Practising rhythm and intonation through dialogues, chants and a song.

Strategies: Using a colour code to identify objects. Acting out the chants, songs and dialogues to learn them. Associating spoken and written words with illustrations.

Unit 2 - My family

Objectives: To identify members of the family. To present one's friends. To complete assessment and self-assessment activities.

Vocabulary: family, dad, mum, brother, sister, granny, grandad, friend.

Language: I love you, (Dad). This is (Freddy). Freddy is my friend. Is it (dad)? This is my family. My granny, my grandad, my mum, my dad, my sister and me! Sorry!

Pronunciation: Pronouncing the unit vocabulary. Using the correct intonation in wh- questions. Practising rhythm and intonation through dialogues, chants and a song.

Strategies: Describing a family tree. Playing games to learn, reinforce and consolidate vocabulary. Using the picture dictionary to consolidate spelling.

Unit 3 - Food

Objectives: To identify food items. To talk about likes and dislikes. To count to five. To complete assessment and self-assessment activities.

Vocabulary: food, apple, banana, orange, biscuit, milk, chicken, ice cream, chocolate, snack, lunch, four, five, hungry, orange.

Language: I like (apples). I'm hungry! Can I have an (apple), please? Here's a biscuit! What's for lunch today? Lunch is ready. I like lunch!

Pronunciation: Pronouncing the unit vocabulary. Using the correct intonation in requests. Practising rhythm and intonation through dialogues, chants and a song.

Strategies: Focusing on context to complete an illustrated scene. Associating spoken words with realia. Playing games to develop observation and memory skills.

Table of contents

Story time 1 - I'm hungry!

Consolidation of units 1-3.

Unit 4 - My body

Objectives: To identify the parts of the body and face. To describe oneself. To count to six. To do assessment and self-assessment activities.

Vocabulary: body, head, arms, legs, feet, hands, eyes, nose, mouth, clown, pirate, robot, six, big, small, brown.

Language: Move your (head). Stamp your feet. Point to the boy. Stop! Wash your hands. I've got blue eyes. He's got (big) eyes. Hello, I'm Cathy. I look like my granny. I've got brown eyes, a small nose and a small mouth. Is it big or small?

Pronunciation: Pronouncing the unit vocabulary. Using the correct intonation in either/or questions. Practising rhythm and intonation through dialogues, chants and a song.

Strategies: Using a colour code to identify parts of the body. Associating spoken and written words with illustrations. Using TPR activities to learn, reinforce and consolidate vocabulary.

Unit 5 - Animals

Objectives: To identify animals. To talk about pets. To identify oneself. To count to eight. To do assessment and self-assessment activities.

Vocabulary: pet, animal, dog, cat, mouse, bird, raccoon, squirrel, fox, rabbit, seven, eight.

Language: This is a (big bird). It says (tweet tweet). What is it? Is it a (mouse)? It's a rabbit. Who are you? I'm (Rocky the raccoon). What is it? A (rabbit). I love animals. I've got a (rabbit).

Pronunciation: Pronouncing the unit vocabulary. Using the correct intonation in wh- questions. Practising rhythm and intonation through dialogues, chants and a song.

Strategies: Using a number code to reinforce vocabulary. Playing games to develop observation and memory skills. Using miming to consolidate vocabulary.

Unit 6 - My holidays

Objectives: To identify holiday clothes and toys. To describe the position of objects. To count to ten. To do assessment and self-assessment activities.

Vocabulary: holidays, rucksack, shorts, sandals, sunhat, sunglasses, ball, electronic game, camera, nine, ten, silly, happy, sad.

Language: Where's my rucksack? Where are my shorts? Under the bed. On your head. We're going away on holiday. Are you happy? Yes, we're happy. He's sad. I'm on holiday with my mum and dad. I'm wearing a sunhat, shorts and sandals. I've got my camera.

Pronunciation: Pronouncing the unit vocabulary. Practising rhythm and intonation through dialogues, chants and a song.

Strategies: Focusing on context to interpret different situations. Using the picture dictionary to consolidate spelling. Using a colour code to classify vocabulary.

Story time 2 - The Gingerbread Man

Consolidation of units 4-6.

Festivals

Celebrating Christmas.
Celebrating Easter.

Introduction

Welcome to **Merry Team**! The following introduction will guide you through the practicalities of using the course and the principles on which it was compiled.

Levels

Merry Team is a six-level course for children studying English at primary level. It has been created to meet the specific needs of young learners, taking into account the cognitive, affective and social development of these age groups.

Duration

Merry Team 1 offers sufficient material for between 60 and 90 lessons, including assessment. Each lesson is expected to take approximately 45 to 60 minutes. However, the teaching notes cater for situations where teachers need to cover more or fewer hours.

General aims

This course aims to teach English as a communicative tool and convey the idea that through English one can access other cultures and other ways of life. The language is always presented through appealing characters and within a familiar context so that children are given the opportunity to use it in real-life situations from the very beginning. In this way they will realise that they can understand and do things in English, thus increasing both their self-esteem and their knowledge of English.

From a linguistic point of view, level 1 aims to provide children with non-verbal strategies for communication as well as core vocabulary that they can recognise. Priority is given to the listening and speaking skills, as oral and aural communication is the most direct form of communication between children. In this level, children will concentrate on pre-reading and pre-writing activities.

Consolidation occurs through frequent revision of the language learnt in previous lessons. This is a key aspect in Merry Team, which also aims to develop children's self-confidence and lead them to communicate in English spontaneously.

Furthermore, this course takes into account the principles of Howard Gardner's Multiple Intelligences theory providing activities which stimulate each type of learning style and intelligence including linguistic, logical-mathematical, spatial, inter-intra-personal, bodily-kinaesthetic and musical. This will help the children acquire the language faster and more effectively.

While developing our material, we have kept in mind some factors which may be common to primary classrooms in many countries. The main ones appear to be crowded conditions, lack of resources, diversity among teachers (specialists who have had little experience working with children versus experienced non-specialists), diversity among pupils (different backgrounds, levels of abilities, etc.) and variations in the numbers of hours per week.

The syllabus of Merry Team is based on the Common European Framework for Language Learning for A1+ (Basic) users.

Introduction

DIDACTICS

Merry Team has been developed in line with the following pedagogical principles:

Pupil-centred approach

Children acquire knowledge based on their own experience, through a complex interactive process involving themselves, the materials and the teacher who links the two. Merry Team contains varied activities which are centred on the pupil and are appropriate to the conceptual and cognitive development of children between the ages of 6 and 12. This approach means that children learn in a meaningful way. It also means that teachers play many different roles: as helpers, monitors, observers, instructors and mediators.

Global approach

In primary education, English is not an isolated subject, but forms part of a comprehensive curriculum of interrelated areas. Merry Team uses the same types of strategies as are covered in other subjects, such as handling materials, observing, predicting, sequencing, grouping and discriminating, amongst many others. Moreover, pupils are called upon to apply different types of intelligences to the tasks involved in language learning and problem solving.

Topics

Each unit of the book develops around a specific topic. All the topics have been chosen to reflect the age and developing interests of the children and cover aspects of the real world as well as imaginative themes. In Merry Team 1, the topics are child centred, thus focus on their immediate world and daily experience.
Apart from the core units, there are additional stories and festivals to consolidate structures and vocabulary and develop different types of skills and intelligences. Teachers decide whether to use them or not, depending on the time they have.

Progress and skills

Merry Team offers thorough coverage of structures, functions, vocabulary and pronunciation. Its syllabus is based on graded structures and vocabulary, and develops all four skills (reading, writing, listening and speaking) through a variety of communicative tasks, while regularly recycling vocabulary and language patterns.

COURSE COMPONENTS OF LEVEL 1

Level 1 comprises a Pupil's Book, an Activity Book with audio CD, a Teacher's Guide, audio material, flashcards, a DVD with animated stories and Rocky's puppet.

For the pupil
- Pupil's Book
- Activity Book + audio CD with stories and songs

Pupil's Book 1

It contains an introductory unit, 6 core units, 2 consolidation units presented as stories and 2 festivals (Christmas and Easter). There is also a revision page, a sticker section in the middle of the book and 3 cut-out pages at the end.
Each topic is developed through the P-P-P-P-model (presentation, practice, production, personalisation).
At the end of each unit, pupils do the Unit Test (Teacher's Guide pp. 87-98) and record their progress with the help of their teacher.

Activity Book 1 + audio CD

This is an attractive, fully-coloured book that contains the practice work for all the units in the Pupil's Book and a Picture Dictionary section which can be used at the end of each unit to revise the basic vocabulary presented in the unit. In this section pupils have the opportunity to develop pre-reading and pre-writing skills.

Note: The cut-outs needed for some activities can be photocopied from pp. 101-104 of this Guide.

The audio CD contains the chants, the stories and songs in the Pupil's Book.

Teacher's Resource Pack

• Teacher's Guide
• Class audio CD
• 64 Flashcards
• DVD (level 1 and 2)
• Rocky's Puppet

The **Teacher's Guide** provides:
• step-by-step lesson plans with suggested reinforcement and extension activities
• keys to the exercises
• the audio scripts of all the listening activities, chants, stories and songs in the Pupil's Book
• a Resource File with ideas for games and extra activities
• 6 photocopiable Unit Tests with keys
• a photocopiable Formative assessment chart
• a photocopiable End of unit assessment chart
• a photocopiable Cut-out section for the Activity Book.

The **Class audio CD** includes all the recordings for the listening activities in the Pupil's Book.

The **Pupil's audio CD** includes the chants, songs and dialogues, all of which are necessary for home study.

Flashcards

The flashcards show the vocabulary presented in each unit and are colour coded in lexical sets, each one corresponding to the unit they refer to.
The flashcards can be used for presentation, revision, additional practice and a variety of stimulating games.

GETTING TO KNOW MERRY TEAM 1

Unit Structure

Except for Unit 0 which is made up of an introductory double page, each unit consists of 8 pages following a regular pattern of 9 lessons:

Lessons 1 and 2

Objectives: presentation of the new lexical items and structures in context. This spread will also help develop observation and oral comprehension skills.
Page 1: Let's chant!
Rocky and his friends present the vocabulary in context through a chant. Pupils complete the illustrated scene with a sticker.

Introduction

Page 2: Listen, trace and colour.
This short activity is aimed to reinforce the target vocabulary and develop fine motor skills.

Lesson 3
Objectives: presentation of a song to recycle and broaden the topic vocabulary. Pupils will learn vocabulary, common expressions (as receptive vocabulary) and will be introduced to the rhythm of English.
Page 3: Let's sing and do!
The song is presented through an illustrated scene with characters and relevant vocabulary. At the bottom of the page there is a picture dictionary presenting the new words.

Lesson 4
Objectives: reinforcement of the unit vocabulary through a pen-to-paper activity and development of observation and fine motor skills.
Page 4: The title depends on the activity, which is usually a maze, a puzzle or a matching exercise.

Lesson 5
Objectives: associating words and pictures to revise and recycle the language seen in the unit through a comic.
Page 5: Let's listen!
A comic featuring Rocky & his friends. The dialogues are in the form of a chant to help retention.

Lesson 6
Objectives: revision and consolidation of the unit vocabulary through a game, development of spoken interaction, fine motor skills, pre-reading, observation and memory skills.
Page 6: Let's play Bingo!
This page features an interactive Bingo grid which pupils complete with stickers.

Lesson 7
Objectives: development of fine motor skills, revision of the unit vocabulary and development of spoken interaction through a craftwork activity.
Activity Book Page: Stick, draw and say.
Pupils carry out this hands-on activity using the the photocopiable cut-outs provided in this guide.

Lesson 8
Objectives: associating spoken words with pictures, development of listening comprehension skills and language transferal into the real world.
Page 7: My world!
This page provides an opportunity for the children to bring closer the language studied in the book. The presentation is done through photos about the world the children are familiar with.

Lesson 9
Objectives: revision of the unit content, development of pre-reading and pre-writing skills; assessment and self-assessment activities.
Page 8: My Turn!
In this page pupils can express themselves through drawings and a simple writing activity. At the end they can stick the end-of-unit sticker in the box.

Festivals

In Merry Team 1 the topics of the festivals are Christmas and Easter. They are designed to be used at the appropriate time of year and the language content reflects the progress pupils should have made by then. Each festival page includes a song and hands-on activity.

Stories

Each story is self-contained and consolidates the language learnt in the preceding units. Stories have been included for the children's enjoyment and as a springboard for additional activities such as dramatisation. Stories are useful in that the story formula, which children are familiar with in their own language, helps them understand the new language and gives them a reason for doing so.

Chants

Merry Team 1 contains a variety of chants aimed to help pupils familiarise with the pronunciation, rhythm and intonation of English.

Songs

Songs provide an opportunity for children to revise and learn new words and structures. Furthermore, not only do they help pupils remember the language but they also play an important role in the development of an accurate pronunciation.

Cross-cultural pages

The My world! pages provide an opportunity for pupils to compare the lives of other children with their own. They are then encouraged to speak, draw and write about themselves.

Personalisation

The My turn! pages provide activities which allow pupils to think about themselves and use the language in a more personal way. This is achieved by drawing, speaking and writing about their own families, friends, pets, preferences and so forth.

Testing and assessment

Assessment is an integral part of language-learning. Its purpose is to monitor progress and how this occurs so as to allow for adjustments in the teaching practice, if necessary.

At the end of each unit, pupils recycle and further consolidate the language they have learnt by completing the My turn! section in the Pupil's Book and the Listen and find! section, as well as the Picture Dictionary page for the unit, in the Activity Book.

The Assessment charts on pp. 99-100 of this Guide are intended to help the teacher organise formative assessment.

The photocopiable Unit Tests at the end of this Guide provide an opportunity for a more formal assessment.

The testing and assessment in Merry Team follow the guidelines set out by the Common European Framework for Languages: Learning, Teaching, Assessment.

http://www.coe.int/T/DG4/Portfolio/documents/0521803136txt.pdf

Unit 0 — Hello!

LESSON 1
Hello! (pp. 2-3)

Objectives: Meet Rocky, Suzy and Freddy. Introduce some simple greetings. Develop fine motor skills.
Language focus: Hello! Hello, my friends. I'm (Rocky).
Target vocabulary: Rocky, Freddy, Suzy.
Materials: Rocky's puppet. Flashcards. Class CD.

Warm-up
Introduce yourself and Rocky.

Wave and say: Hello, I'm (your name)! Hello! Invite the class to say Hello! to you. Repeat this twice.
Go up to a child and shake hands while you say: Hello, I'm (your name). Elicit Hello! I'm (pupil's name). Do this with as many pupils as possible.
Finally read and explain the title of the unit.

1 🔊 Let's chant. (p. 2)
Introduce the characters.

Pupils' books closed. Stick the flashcards of the characters on the board one by one and introduce them. Alternatively you can use the puppet to present Rocky. Say: Look, this is Rocky. Encourage pupils to say: Hello, Rocky! Do the same with Suzy and Freddy. Remove the flashcards from the board and stick them on different walls. Elicit the characters' names each time.
Pupils point to the characters you indicate. Say: Point to (Suzy)! Repeat several times, increasing the speed and varying the order of the instructions. Then point to the flashcards at random and elicit the characters' names.
Play track 2 of the class CD and encourage pupils to listen and look at you while you point to the characters in your book. Say: Listen!

Audio script

ROCKY Hello, hello,
       I'm Rocky.
       I'm Rocky,
       Hello, my friends!

SUZY   Hello, hello,
       I'm Suzy.
       I'm Suzy,
       Hello, my friends!

FREDDY Hello, hello,
       I'm Freddy.
       I'm Freddy,
       Hello, my friends!

Pupils' books open. Focus pupils' attention on page 2. Play track 2 again and invite them to listen, point to each character on the page and say the appropriate greeting.
Play the chant again, doing one of the following activities each time: **1** Pupils point to the characters in their books. Say: Listen and point. **2** Pupils wave their hands when they hear the word hello! **3** Pause after each verse and encourage pupils to respond. Say: Listen and say hello!

Round-up
A game to consolidate the characters' names.

Show the character's flashcards one by one and say: Hello, I'm … Elicit the appropriate name each time and encourage pupils to respond Hello, (Rocky)! Encourage pupils to stand up one by one, wave their hand and say: Hello, I'm (Maria)! The rest of the class responds: Hello, (Maria)! while they wave back.

Activity Book (p. 2)

Find and colour.
Pupils identify a character.

Pupils go to page 2 of the Activity book. In L1, explain

that they are going to find and colour Rocky. First ask them to trace the outline of the character on the page with their finger. Say: Find Rocky. Then tell them to choose any colour they like. Say: Colour Rocky.

Reinforcement activity: Say the chant to an individual pupil. Encourage him/her to reply with the character's name for example: Hello, (Rocky)! Repeat with the other verses and different pupils.

Extension activity: Play the 'Echo Game' with the whole class using the vocabulary of the unit (Resource File, Flashcard game 2, p. 78).

LESSON 2
Hello! (pp. 2-3)

> **Objectives:** Present colours. Reinforce the characters' names and some greetings. Develop observation skills.
> **Language focus:** Hello! Hello, my friends. I'm (Rocky).
> **Target vocabulary:** red, yellow, blue, green.
> **Vocabulary (revision):** Rocky, Suzy, Freddy, Hello, I'm…
> **Materials:** Flashcards of the characters. Flashcards of the colours. Class CD. Red, yellow and blue crayons.

Warm-up
Revise the chant of the previous lesson.

Begin the lesson by chanting and acting out the unit chant (page 2). Encourage everyone to join in. Show the flashcards of the characters one by one and encourage pupils to greet them. Pupils say for example: Hello, (Rocky)!

1 Let's chant! (pp. 2-3)
Present and practise colours.

Pupils' books open. Focus pupils' attention on pages

2 and 3. Point to the balloons and identify the colours. Say: Look. This is red … blue … yellow. Then point to the trees and bushes and say: Look. This is green. Point to the colours at random and ask pupils to say the words chorally or individually.
Say the colour of each balloon and elicit the character. Say: Red and elicit: Rocky; blue / Suzy; yellow / Freddy. Then do the opposite, naming the characters and eliciting the colours.
Ask pupils to take out the following crayons: red, blue, yellow and green. Show them the crayons one by one and say the colours: This is (red).
Ask pupils to follow your instructions. Say: Show me red … yellow … blue … green. Do this several times, varying the order and the rhythm.
Pupils close their eyes. Remove one crayon and show pupils the remaining three. Encourage them to say which crayon is missing. Repeat this game several times.

2 Join and say. (p. 3)
Pupils identify the characters by their silhouettes.

Focus pupils' attention on the character's names and read them. Pupils point to the characters in their books.
Explain the task. Pupils have to join the characters with their silhouettes.
When they have finished, name each character and ask pupils to identify the colour of the corresponding silhouette: Rocky – red, Suzy – blue, Freddy – yellow.

Round-up
A game to revise colours.

Pupils' books closed. Play 'Touch red' with the whole class using the vocabulary of the unit (Resource File, TPR game 1, p. 77).

Activity Book (p. 3)

Join, trace and colour.
Developing fine motor and pre-writing skills.

Focus the pupils' attention on the crayons. Point to each one and elicit the colour. Ask pupils to take out the same crayons. Check these by saying: Show me

Hello !

red … blue … yellow.
Show the first crayon on the left. Trace the path joining it to Rocky with your finger. Then ask pupils to colour Rocky's T-shirt red and trace Rocky's name.
Pupils do the same with the blue and yellow crayons. Go round the room to help pupils with the activity. Check the task by showing pupils the completed page. Encourage them to say: Rocky – red, Suzy – yellow, Freddy – blue.

Reinforcement activity: Play ' Correct Rocky!' with the class, using the flashcards of the characters and the colours (Resource File, Flashcard game 3, p. 78).

Extension activity: Play 'Chinese Whispers' with the whole class using the vocabulary of the unit (Resource File, Flashcard game 1, p. 78).

My room

LESSON 1

My room (pp. 4-5)

Objectives: Recognise and name some items of furniture. Develop fine motor skills. Reinforce the colours and the characters' names.
Language focus: This is my (table). They are my friends.
Target vocabulary: table, chair, window, door.
Vocabulary (revision): Hello, Rocky, Suzy, Freddy, red, blue, yellow, green.
Materials: Flashcards, class CD.

Warm-up

Revising 'hello!' and the characters' names.

Stick the flashcards of Rocky, Freddy and Suzy on the board one by one, and elicit their names.
Point to Rocky, clap your hands rhythmically and chant out: Hello, Rocky, hello! Encourage pupils to repeat. Do the same with Suzy and Freddy.
Point to one pupil and ask the rest of the class to turn towards him or her, clap their hands and chant out the greeting. Do this with as many pupils as possible.
Finally read and explain the title of the unit.

Pre-listening activities (pp. 4-5)

Present items of furniture and revise the characters.

Pupils' books closed. Stick the flashcards of the table, chair, door and window on the board one by one. Say: Look, this is a (table). Encourage pupils to repeat chorally and individually.
Remove the flashcards from the board and stick them on different walls. Pupils point to the items of furniture you say. Say: Point to (the table)! Repeat several times, increasing the speed and varying the order of the instructions.

Pupils' books open. Focus pupils' attention on the scene. Point to the character and say: Look! This is…

Elicit: Rocky. In L1 explain that he is in his room. Pupils observe the scene and try to predict who or what is missing. Ask: Where's Freddy? And Suzy? Confirm that Freddy and Suzy are missing. Show them the sticker in the middle of the book. Pupils peel it off and stick it on page 5 to complete the scene.

1 [03] Let's chant! (pp. 4-5)

Practising the pronunciation of the new words.

Pupils' books open. Focus pupils' attention on the illustration and describe what's happening: Rocky is showing us his room and his friends.
Point to the table and say: This is a table. Elicit its colour: Red. Do the same with the chair, door and window.
Present the chant with the CD and the book.
Encourage pupils to listen and look at you while you point in your book. Say: Listen!

Audio script

ROCKY This is my table
And my chair!
My table and my chair!

This is my window
And my door!
My window and my door!

Table, chair,
Window, door!

And they are…
They are my friends!!!

Play the chant again doing one of the following activities:
- Pupils point to the items of furniture in their books. Say: Listen and point.
- Pupils point to Suzy and Freddy when they hear the word friends. Say: Listen and point. Pause after each verse and encourage pupils to repeat the words. Say: Listen and repeat!

1 My room

Round-up

Activity Book (p. 4)

Find, colour and say.
Identifying and pronouncing some items of furniture.

Pupils go to page 4 of the Activity Book. Tell them that they are going to find and colour some items of furniture in the drawing. First, they identify the colour of each picture at the top. Say: table and elicit: blue; chair/red; window/green. Then, they find out the shapes of the items of furniture in the drawing and colour them in.

Reinforcement activity: Pupils point to these items of furniture in the classroom. Say: Point to the (window).

Extension activity: Play 'What is it?' using the flashcards. (Resource File, Flashcard game 5, p. 79)

LESSON 2

My room (pp. 4-5)

> **Objectives:** Reinforce items of furniture. Develop fine motor skills. Solve a puzzle. Develop pre-reading and pre-writing skills.
> **Language focus:** This is my (window).
> **Vocabulary (revision):** red, yellow, blue, green, table, chair, window, door.
> **Materials:** Flashcards. Red, blue, green and yellow crayons. Class CD.

Warm-up
Revise the chant on page 4.

Begin the lesson by chanting and acting out the unit chant. Play the CD and encourage everyone to join in.

Pupils' books open. Focus pupils' attention on the illustration. Play the CD again, asking them to follow the chant and point to the items of furniture as they are named.

2 Listen, trace and colour. (p. 5)
Developing listening, observation and fine motor skills.

Read the words and ask pupils to repeat them.
Ask pupils to take out the following crayons: red, blue, yellow and green. Hold them up one by one and elicit the colours: This is… (red).
Pupils raise up in the air the crayons according to colour you elicit. Say: Show me red … yellow … blue … green. Do this several times, varying the order and the rhythm.
Explain the task and play track 4. Pupils trace and colour each item of furniture according to what they hear. First, they listen and mark the colour of each item with a dot. You can play the CD twice. Then, they finish tracing and colouring the pictures.

Audio script

1   Red! The table is red.

2   Blue! The chair is blue.

3   Yellow! The window is yellow.

4   Green! The door is green.

Go round the room to help pupils. Check their understanding of the vocabulary and of the task by naming each item and eliciting the colour. Say: table and elicit: red. Do the same with chair, window and door. Then double check by saying the colour first and eliciting the corresponding object.

Round-up

Activity Book (p. 5)

Join, trace and say.
Developing observation, pre-writing and speaking skills.

Point to number one and follow the line with your finger in order to show how the two halves of the table match to form the whole picture. Then ask the pupils to trace the word table.
Tell pupils (in L1) to match the two parts of the remaining objects and trace the corresponding words.
Go round the room to help pupils and check the

understanding of the language tackled. You can ask individual pupils to identify and pronounce the objects and the colours.

Reinforcement activity: Play 'Twist around.' Pupils should now be pointing to real items of furniture in the classroom (Resource File, TPR game 5, p. 77).

Extension activity: Play 'What's missing?' using the flashcards of furniture items (Resource File, Flashcard game 4, p. 78).

LESSON 3
Let's sing and do! (p. 6)

> **Objectives:** Present some classroom objects and count to three. Develop listening comprehension skills. Develop pre-reading and pre-writing skills. Sing a song and act it out.
> **Language focus:** Pick up the (pencil). Pick it up, put it down. Up and down.
> **Target vocabulary:** crayon, pencil, book, one, two, three, please, thank you.
> **Vocabulary (revision):** table, chair, door, window , red, yellow, blue, green.
> **Materials:** Flashcards. A pencil, a crayon and a book. Class CD.

Warm-up
A TPR activity to present 'up' and 'down.'

Count on your fingers in time and do the actions as you chant the following lines quite slowly:
Stand up! Stand up!
One, two, three,
Sit down! Sit down!
Encourage pupils to repeat the chant, counting on their fingers and doing the actions. Repeat the chant, speeding up the rhythm.

Pre-listening activity
A TPR activity to prepare for the song.

Pupils' books closed. Show the following classroom objects: a book, a pencil and a crayon. Pick up each item and say the word. Encourage pupils to repeat chorally and individually. Then point to the objects in random order and elicit the words.
Play 'Twist around' using classroom objects (Resource File, TPR game 5, page 77).

1 05 **Let's sing and do! (p. 6)**
Pupils sing the unit song and act it out.

Pupils' books open. Focus pupils' attention on page 6. Pupils point to the classroom objects as you name them. Say: Point to the (pencil)!
Present the song using the CD and the book. Pupils listen and look at the pictures as you point to them in your book. Say: Listen to the song!

Audio script

MAN   One, two, three
        Pick up the pencil,
        Pick up the pencil, please!

CHORUS Pick it up,
        Put it down!
        Up and down,
        Up and down!

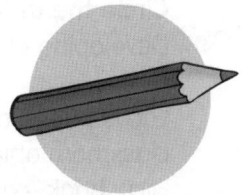

MAN   One, two, three
        Pick up the crayon,
        Pick up the crayon, please!

CHORUS Pick it up,
        Put it down!
        Up and down,
        Up and down!

MAN   One, two, three
        Pick up the book,
        Pick up the book, please!

CHORUS Pick it up,
        Put it down!
        Up and down,
        Up and down!

1 My room

Point out that to ask for things politely they have to say please. Teach or revise the expression thank you.
Ask pupils to place a pencil, a crayon and a book on their desks. Check that they have the correct items saying: Show me the (pencil).
Play the song again doing one of the following activities each time: **1** Pupils listen to the song pointing to each object in their books. Say: Listen and point. **2** Pupils do the actions with you using real objects. Say: Listen and do! **3** Pupils do the actions and sing along. Say: Sing and do! **4** Divide the class into three groups. Each group sings and acts out one stanza while the other two clap in time.
Finally, read the words at the bottom of the page and ask pupils to repeat them. Then repeat the words at random and ask pupils to point to the words you say.

Round-up

Activity Book (p. 6)

Circle the differences and trace.
Developing observation and fine motor skills.

Focus pupils' attention on picture A. Pupils identify the classroom objects and the colours, then count them.
Elicit: book – one, yellow; crayons – one, two, red; pencils – one, two, three, blue.
Do the same with picture B. Ask pupils to circle the differences and show them how to do.
Check their work by pointing to and saying the differences, for example: The book is yellow in picture A. The book is blue in picture B.
At the end, pupils trace the words at the bottom of the page.

Reinforcement activity: Play 'Touch red.' (Resource File, TPR game 1, p. 77)

Extension activity: Play 'What's missing?' using the flashcards. (Resource File, Flashcard game 4, p. 78)

LESSON 4

Join and say. (p. 7)

Objectives: Sing the song and act it out. Reinforce the vocabulary of the unit. Practise counting to three. Develop observation and fine motor skills.
Language focus: Pick up the (pencil). Pick it up, put it down. Up and down.
Vocabulary (revision): table, chair, door, window, crayon, book, one, two, three, red, yellow, blue, green.
Materials: Flashcards, class CD.

Warm-up
Revise the song on page 6.

Ask pupils to place a pencil, a crayon and a book on their desks. Check that they have the correct items by saying: Show me the (pencil).
Begin the lesson by singing and acting out the song.
Play the CD. Encourage everyone to join in and do the actions using the classroom objects they have learnt.

Preparing for the 'Join and say' activity
Revise counting to three and the vocabulary.

Show the flashcards one by one and elicit the words. Play 'Sequences.' (Resource File, Flashcards game 7, p. 79)
Practise counting using the vocabulary of the unit.
Point to the windows in the room and count them from 1 to 3. Say: One, two, three windows. Do the same with other items. Encourage pupils to count with you.
Finally, ask different pupils to count the objects you show them, for example: 2 crayons, 1 book, 3 pencils, etc.

Join and say. (p. 7)
Develop observation and speaking skills.

Pupils take out red, blue and yellow crayons. Ask them to hold up the correct crayon when you say: Show me (red).

Focus their attention on the page. Point to the birds on the left. Explain in L1 that they have lost their classroom objects on the right and need help to find them.
Point to the first bird and follow the path with your finger down to the red pencils on the right. Count and say: One, two, three pencils – red.
Pupils join the first bird and the pencils with a red crayon. When they have finished, ask them to do the same with the remaining birds using a blue crayon for the second bird and a yellow one for the third bird.
While pupils are working, go round the class and ask individual pupils to identify the classroom objects, the colours and count them.
Check their work by pointing and saying: First bird… and help pupils say: Three pencils – red. Do the same with the other birds.

Round-up
Verify comprehension of the unit vocabulary.

Play 'Pass it on' using classroom objects of different colours. Say: Show me the (yellow crayon)! Show me the (red book)! (Resource File, TPR game 3, p. 77)

Reinforcement activity: Play 'Rocky says' using the following instructions: Point to a (window)! Pick up a (crayon)! Put down a (crayon)! (Resource File, TPR game 2, p. 77)

Extension activity: Play 'Follow the leader' using the following instructions: Let's play 'Follow the leader'! One, two, three, point to a (window)! One, two three, point to (red)! etc. (Resource File, Flashcard game 10, p. 79)

LESSON 5
Let's listen! (p. 8)

> **Objectives:** Associate spoken words with pictures. Develop observation skills. Revise vocabulary. Develop awareness of possible dangers.
> **Language focus:** Hello, my friends! Come in and close the door! Come on to bed!
> **Target vocabulary:** bed.
> **Vocabulary (revision):** table, chair, door, window, crayon, book, red, yellow, blue, green.
> **Materials:** Flashcards, class CD, sheets of paper (extension activity).

Warm-up
Revise colours and vocabulary.

Play 'Pass it on' using classroom objects of different colours. Say: Show me the (yellow crayon)! Show me the (red book)! (Resource File, Class game 3, p. 77)

Pre-listening activity
Present the word 'bed' and prepare students for the comic.

Pupils' books closed. Draw a bed on the board and ask pupils to identify it in L1. Then ask: What's this? and say: A bed. Pupils repeat the word several times.
Draw the outline of a room on the board and stick the following flashcards in the room: door, window, table and chair. Point to each flashcard and say the words. Pupils repeat chorally and individually. Then point to the items of furniture at random and elicit the words.

Let's listen! (p. 8)
Present the vocabulary in context.

Focus pupils' attention on the scene. In L1, ask them to describe what is happening in the frames: Freddy and Suzy are visiting Rocky. Freddy has an accident.
Tell pupils to point to the bed, the door, Rocky, Suzy and Freddy. Say: Point to the bed! Point to (Rocky). Present the comic using the CD and the book. Say: Listen and look at the pictures!

My room

Audio script

1	ROCKY	Hello, my friends, hello!
	SUZY AND FREDDY	Hello, Rocky. Hello!

2	ROCKY	Come in and close the door!

3		SLAM!!!

4	FREDDY	Ouch, ouch!
	ROCKY	Come on the bed, Freddy. On the bed!

5	ROCKY AND SUZY	Poor Freddy! Poor friend!

6	SUZY	Don't slam the door! Close it slowly!

Make sure that pupils understand the dialogues. Then play the comic again doing one of the following activities each time: **1** Pupils follow the comic in their books, pointing to each frame in turn. Say: Listen and point. **2** Pupils wave their hands when they hear the word 'Hello!' Say: Listen and do! **3** Play the CD again with pauses for them to repeat, chorally or individually. Check their pronunciation and intonation.

Round-up

Pupils act out the comic.

Divide the class into three groups and assign the roles of Rocky, Suzy and Freddy. Give each group the flashcard of one character.
Play the CD again, with pauses after each line so that each group can repeat it and mime the actions. If you have time, swap roles and repeat the activity.

Reinforcement activity: Read out different lines from the comic and elicit the character's name each time.

Extension activity: Ask pupils to draw an accident that could happen if they slammed a door. On the board, write: Don't slam the door! Pupils copy the sentence at the top of their pictures. Collect the drawings and make a display. When you take down the display, help pupils store their drawings in their Language Portfolio.

LESSON 6
Let's play Bingo! (p. 9)

Objectives: Revise and consolidate the vocabulary of this unit. Develop spoken interaction. Develop fine motor skills. Develop pre-reading, observation and memory skills.
Language focus: A red (pencil).
Vocabulary (revision): window, door, bed, table, chair, pencil, crayon, book. Colours.
Materials: Flashcards. Stickers. Nine tokens (or scraps of paper) per pupil to play Bingo. Formative assessment sheet (Resource File, p. 99).

Warm-up
Revise the unit vocabulary.

Show the unit flashcards one by one and elicit the words as you stick them on the left-hand side of the board. Do the same with the colour flashcards and stick them on the right-hand side.
Say: A red pencil. Take both flashcards and stick them together. Stick the colour flashcard first and then the object one. Repeat: A red pencil. Give more examples with the rest of the flashcards. Pupils repeat chorally or individually.
Put the flashcards back in their original positions. Call different pupils to the board and say, for example: A yellow table. The pupil selects the appropriate flashcards and stick them together. Encourage him/her to say the words. Repeat the procedure several times with different pupils.

Preparing for the Bingo! (p. 9 and stickers)
Pupils complete the Bingo grid with stickers.

Focus pupils' attention on the page. Tell them that, in order to play Bingo, they have to complete the grid by sticking the appropriate stickers in the white circles. Pupils go to the stickers page and look for the yellow table. When they find it, they peel it off and go back to page 9. Ask them to stick it in any of the white circles. Do the same with the stickers of the green crayon and the red book.

Let's play Bingo! (p. 9)
Check comprehension of the unit vocabulary.

Focus pupils' attention on the page. Ask them to identify some of the objects in the squares. Point and ask: What's this? Elicit: A (window). What colour is it? Elicit: (Yellow). Confirm by saying: A yellow window. Pupils repeat chorally or individually.
In L1, ask them how they play Bingo! Confirm that they have to cover the squares when they hear the words. When all the squares are covered they say: Bingo! Hand out nine tokens to each pupil. Say the words at random and slowly, twice. For example: A blue door. When the game is over, play again, asking a pupil to help you.

Round-up

Developing spoken interaction through the Bingo!

Pupils play in pairs. One says the words and the other covers them. Then they swap roles. They can say only the object: A book! or the object and its colour: A red book! Go round the room to help them, if necessary, and/or assess speaking skills using the Formative assessment sheet (Resource File, p. 99).

Reinforcement activity: Play the 'Echo Game' with the unit flashcards (Resource File, Flashcard game 2, p. 78).

Extension activity: Give pupils a few moments to memorise the page, focusing primarily on the colours. Pupils' books closed, ask: What colour is the (chair)? Elicit: Red. Pupils check the answers by looking at the page.

LESSON 7
Stick, draw and say.
Activity Book (p. 7)

Objectives: Develop fine motor skills. Revise the unit vocabulary. Develop spoken interaction.
Language focus : Is it a (table)?
Vocabulary (revision): bed, chair, table, door, window, book, pencil crayon. Colours.
Materials: Flashcards. Photocopies of Cut-out (p. 101). Your completed page 7 from the Activity Book.

Warm-up
Revise the unit vocabulary and the song on page 6.

Ask pupils to place a pencil, a crayon and a book on their desks. Check that they have the correct items by saying: Show me the (pencil).
Begin the lesson by singing and acting out the song on page 6. Play the CD. Encourage everyone to join in and do the actions using the classroom objects.

Stick, draw and say.
Developing spoken interaction.

Focus pupils' attention on the page. Say: This is a house. Point to the window and ask: What's this? Elicit: A window. Ask them to identify what is missing in this house: The door.
Explain that they are going to complete the house by sticking the door on it. Show them your finished page.
Hand out the photocopies of page 101. Ask them to cut it out and colour it using a colour that they know in English.
Pupils go back to page 7. Show them how to fold the flap in the door and stick it to the house on the AB page.
When they finish, they open the door and draw and colour one of the following items inside: a bed, a chair or a table. They can also draw a character if

1 My room

they wish. Tell them not to show their page to anyone.

Guessing game
Developing spoken interaction.

Play this guessing game with different pupils. Point to the closed door on the page and ask: Is it a (bed)? Elicit: Yes or No. Once pupils guess the item of furniture they can also guess the colour. Ask: Is it (red)?
Pupils play in pairs. Go round the room in order to give any necessary help and/or assess speaking skills using the Formative assessment sheet (Resource File, p. 99).

Round-up

Display the pupils' finished pages.

Prepare a display of the Activity Book pages so that pupils can see their classmates' work.

Reinforcement activity: Play 'Pass it on' (Resource File, Class game 3, p. 77).

Extension activity: Collect all the Activity Books, choose one at random, go to page 7 and say:
In this house there is a red bed. The pupil, or pupils, who have drawn a red bed stand up and say: It's my bed.

LESSON 8
My world! (p. 10)

> **Objectives:** Associate spoken words with pictures. Develop listening comprehension skills. Revise vocabulary. Transfer the new language into an authentic context.
> **Language focus:** This is my room. I've got a table and a chair.
> **Vocabulary (revision):** Bed, table, chair, door, window. Colours.
> **Materials:** Flashcards. Class CD.

Warm-up
Revise the vocabulary.

Show the flashcards of the unit, characters and colours one by one and elicit the words. Then play 'Pass the flashcards' using all the flashcards. (Resource File, Flashcard game 6, p. 79)

Listen and point. (p. 10)
Developing listening comprehension.

Focus pupils' attention on the page. Point to the boy and say: Look, this is his room! Ask pupils to point to the appropriate items as you name them. Say: Point to the (table).
Then play 'Touch red' using the photo on the page. (Resource File, Class game 1, p. 77)
Finally invite pupils to listen to the child speaking about his room. Play the CD.

Audio script

BOY   This is my room!
      I've got a table and two chairs.
      And look, this is my bed!

Play the CD again doing one of the following activities each time: **1** Pupils listen to the CD and point to the items of furniture as they hear the words. Say: Listen and point. **2** Play the CD again with pauses for them to repeat, chorally or individually. Check their pronunciation and intonation, stressing the /s/ of the plural.

Round-up

Activity Book (p. 8)

Draw and say.
Revising colours and items of furniture.

Ask pupils to take out their green, blue and yellow crayons. Hold them up one by one and elicit the colours.
Ask pupils to follow your instructions. Say: Show me green … yellow … blue.
Explain the task. Pupils trace and colour each item of furniture. Elicit the colour. Say: The table is … green. The chair is … yellow. The bed is … blue.
Go round the room to help pupils with the activity. Ask individual pupils to identify the items and the colours.

Reinforcement activity: Play 'Vanishing pictures' with the unit flashcards. (Resource File, Flashcards game 11, p. 79)

Extension activity: Help pupils create a display with photos of real bedrooms. These can be cut out of magazines and mounted on poster paper. Write 'Rooms' as the poster title. Then ask different pupils to point to a bedroom in the poster and identify the items they can name in English. Help them say, for example: This is a window. This is a chair. This is a blue chair.

LESSON 9
My turn! (p. 11)

Objectives: Revise and consolidate the vocabulary and structures of Unit 1. Revise the unit song. Develop listening skills. Develop pre-reading and pre-writing skills. Assessment and self-assessment progress.
Language (revision): Structures of the unit.
Vocabulary (revision): Unit vocabulary.
Materials: Five tokens or scraps of paper per child. Class CD. Flashcards.

Warm-up
Revise the song and the unit vocabulary.

Ask pupils to place a pencil, a crayon and a book on their desks. Check that they have the correct items by saying: Show me the (pencil).
Begin the lesson by singing and acting out the unit song (p. 6). Encourage everyone to join in and do the actions using the classroom objects.

My turn! (p. 11)
Pupils give personal information using the language they have learnt.

Focus pupils' attention on the page. Point to the words at the bottom and read them aloud. Pupils point to the words as they hear them.
Stick the unit flashcards on the board one by one. Elicit each word, then write it under the corresponding flashcard. Then play 'Words and pictures.' (Resource File, Flashcard games 13, p. 80). Leave the flashcards on the board for the next activity.
Focus pupils' attention on the frame. Ask them to draw and colour four items that belong to them and that they can name in English. When they finish, they copy the related words under the pictures.
Go round the room in order to help pupils with the activity. Ask individual pupils to identify the objects and their colours.

My room

Round-up

Activity Book (p. 9)

Pupils listen and identify objects.

Focus pupils' attention on the page and explain the task. Pupils have to put a token or a scrap of paper on one object in each row according to your instructions. Hand out five tokens to each pupil. Point to the first row and say: This is a (table). Repeat twice.
Do the same with the remaining rows of objects, choosing only one item each time.
Check the task by asking different pupils to identify the items they have covered.

End-of-unit sticker
Focus pupils' attention on the empty circle on the right-hand corner of the frame. Then tell pupils that Rocky is happy because they have finished Unit 1 and invite them to peel off Rocky's sticker in the middle of the book and complete page 11.

Reinforcement activity: Repeat the activity on page 9 (AB) using different words.

Extension activity: Pupils work in pairs. One pupil says the words and the other covers them. Then they swap roles.

Picture dictionary
Turn to page 40 of the Activity Book and tell pupils they are going to revise the unit vocabulary orally and in writing. Point to the pictures in order and ask pupils to identify them. Then point to the pictures at random and do the same. Finally, pupils trace over the words.

Testing and Assessment

Unit test
Photocopy Test 1 on pages 87 and 88 and hand out one copy to each pupil. Pupils complete the test individually. Once you have corrected all the tests, return them to pupils and help them check their performance by writing the answers on the board. Record pupils' results on the End of Unit assessment sheet. (Resource File, p. 100)
Make sure they file their tests in their Language Portfolio.

If you need to consolidate or develop the unit further, please turn to the Resource File (page 77).

My family

My family (pp. 12-13)

Objectives: Recognise and name members of the family. Develop fine motor skills.
Language focus: I love you, (Dad).
Target vocabulary: Family, dad, mum, brother, sister.
Vocabulary (revision): Furniture. Classroom objects. Colours.
Materials: Photo of a well-known family showing the father, mother, brother(s) and sister(s). Flashcards of Rocky, dad, mum, brother, sister. Class CD.

Warm-up
Present the new topic.

In L1, tell pupils that in this unit they are going to talk about different families and about their own family. Pin up the photo of the family you have brought and ask pupils to identify the people. Then point to the different members and say: This is dad … mum … brother … sister. Point to each person again and say the corresponding word. Encourage pupils to repeat.

Pre-listening activities. (pp. 12-13)
Present family members.

Pupils' books closed. Draw a large tree with several branches on the board. The branches should spread out on two levels. Stick the flashcards of Rocky's dad and mum on the two top branches, then his brother and sister on a bottom branch, with Rocky in the middle.
Point to each flashcard and identify the family member. Pupils repeat chorally and individually. Then point to the flashcards at random and elicit the words. Remove the flashcards from the board and stick them on different walls. Pupils point to the family members you indicate. Say: Point to (mum)! Repeat several times, increasing the speed and varying the order of the instructions.

Pupils' books open. Focus pupils' attention on the scene. Point to the character and say: Look! This is… . Elicit: Rocky. In L1 explain that he is going to tell us about his family.
Pupils observe the whole scene and try to predict who is missing. Ask: Where's his brother? And his sister? Confirm that Rocky's brother and sister are missing. Show them the sticker in the middle of the book and ask them to peel it off carefully and go back to page 12. Once they are sure of the position, they stick it on the page.

1 **Let's chant. (pp. 12-13)**
Pupils practise the vocabulary.

Pupils' books open. Focus pupils' attention on the scene and describe the situation: Rocky is showing us his family tree.
Ask pupils to point to dad, mum, brother, sister and Rocky.
Present the chant with the CD and the book.
Encourage pupils to listen and look at you while you point at the characters in your book. Say: Listen!

Audio script

ROCKY   Dad, Dad,
           I love you, Dad!

           Mum, Mum,
           I love you, Mum!

           Brother, brother,
           I love you, brother!

           Sister, sister,
           I love you, sister!

           Mum, Dad,
           Brother, sister,
           I love you all!!

Play the chant again, doing one of the following activities each time: **1** Pupils point to the family

My family

members in their books. Say: Listen and point. **2** Pupils open their arms wide when they hear the words: I love you, (Dad)! Say: Listen and do. **3** Pause after each verse and encourage pupils to repeat. Say: Listen and repeat!

Round-up

Activity Book (p. 10)

Find, circle and say.
Developing observation skills and counting.

Pupils go to page 10 of the Activity Book. Point to the baby rabbit in the lower left hand corner of the page. In L1, explain that he is looking for his family. Help pupils find and point to dad, mum, sister and brother. Then they circle each one and say the words aloud. When they have finished, show them the completed page so they can check their work.

Reinforcement activity: Hold up your book to the class. Say the chant on page 12 of the Pupil's Book and point to the pictures in turn. Repeat and invite the pupils to complete your sentences.
Example:
Teacher: Dad, Dad, …
Pupils: I love you, Dad!

Extension activity: Play 'Odd one out' using the following lexical sets: items of furniture, classroom objects, colours and family members. (Resource File, Production game 2, p. 78)

LESSON 2

My family (pp. 12-13)

Objectives: Reinforce family members. Develop fine motor skills. Revise vocabulary from the previous unit. Develop pre-reading and pre-writing skills.
Language focus: I love you (all).
Vocabulary (revision): Dad, Mum, brother, sister, table, chair, window, door, red, yellow, blue, green.
Materials: Flashcards of dad, mum, sister, brother. Flashcards of Unit 1. Red, blue, green and yellow crayons. Class CD. Sheets of paper (extension activity).

Warm-up
Revise the unit chant.

Begin the lesson by chanting and acting out the unit chant. Play the CD and encourage everyone to join in. Show the flashcards of Unit 1, one by one, and elicit the words. Stick them on the board and play 'What's missing?' (Resource File, Flashcards game 4, p. 78).

Pupils' books open. Focus pupils' attention on the double spread. Play the CD again, asking them to follow the chant and point to the family members as they hear them.

2 **Listen, join and say. (p. 13)**
Pupils listen to and practise the pronunciation of family members, classroom objects and colours.

Ask pupils to take out the following crayons: red, blue, yellow and green. Show them the crayons one by one and elicit the colours: This is… (red).
Explain the task: pupils join the family members to the items they own, using a crayon of the same colour. Identify the characters and the objects first, then play Track 9.

Audio script

1 Dad – book
   Dad's got a book.

2 sister – chair
   Sister's got a chair.

3 brother – pencil
   Brother's got a pencil.

4 Mum – crayon
   Mum's got a crayon.

Go round the room to help pupils with the activity. Check the task by naming each item and eliciting the owner. Say: Pencil and elicit: Brother. Do the same with the book, crayon and chair. Then reverse the procedure, saying the colour first and eliciting the corresponding item and owner, for example: green … chair … sister.

Round-up

Activity Book (p. 11)

Find, colour and trace. Who is it?
Pupils observe and practise new vocabulary.

Point to the words at the top of the page and read them aloud while pointing to the corresponding characters. Pupils point and repeat, then they trace each word in pencil.
Focus attention on the grid and explain (in L1) that one of these four characters is hidden in the drawing. The task is to find and colour it. Go round the room to help pupils with the activity. When they finish, hold up the finished page so that they can check their work, and confirm that the hidden character is mum.

Reinforcement activity: Play the 'Echo game' using the family vocabulary. (Resource File, Flashcards game 2, p. 78)

Extension activity: Hand out sheets of paper and ask pupils to draw a family of animals and label each member. Collect the drawings and make a display. When you take down the display, help pupils store their drawings in their Language Portfolio.

LESSON 3
Let's sing and do! (p. 14)

Objectives: Present more family vocabulary. Develop listening comprehension skills. Develop reading and writing skills. Sing the song and act it out.
Language focus: This is (Freddy). Freddy is my friend.
Target vocabulary: granny, grandad, friend.
Vocabulary (revision): Dad, Mum, brother, sister, hello.
Materials: Unit 2 flashcards. Freddy and Suzy flashcards. Class CD.

Warm-up
Present the word 'friend'.

Demonstrate the following activity with a pupil. Shake hands and say: Hello, (Daniel). Elicit hello and a handshake from the pupil. Look at him and say: You are my friend!
Ask pupils to stand in pairs while you chant the following lines:

Hello, hello, [pupils shake hands]
How are you?
Hello, hello, [pupils shake hands]
You are my friend!

Pre-listening activity
Present 'granny' and 'grandad.'

Pupils' books closed. Show the pupils the flashcards of Rocky's granny and grandad. In L1, ask them how they are related to Rocky. Confirm that they are either his mum's parents or his dad's parents.
Stick the flashcards on the board and present the words. Pupils repeat chorally and individually.

1 10 **Let's sing and do! (p. 14)**
Pupils sing and act out a song.

Pupils' books open. Focus pupils' attention on page 14. Pupils point to the characters as you name them.

My family

Say: Point to (granny)!
Present the song using the CD and the book. Pupils listen and look at the pictures as you point in your book. Say: Listen to the song!

Audio script

ROCKY	Granny, granny, This is Freddy, Freddy is my friend!
GRANNY	Hello, Freddy, Hello, hello!
ROCKY	Grandad, grandad, This is Suzy, Suzy is my friend!
GRANDAD	Hello, Suzy, Hello, hello!
ROCKY	Freddy and Suzy. They are my friends!

Play the song again, doing one of the following activities each time: **1** Pupils follow the song in their books, pointing to each character in turn. Say: Listen and point. **2** Pupils wave when they hear the hello. Say: Listen and do! **3** Divide the class into three groups: Rocky, granny and grandad. Hand out Freddy's and Suzy's flashcards to the Rocky group. Pupils in this group sing the first stanza while waving Freddy's flashcard. The Granny group replies with the first chorus. The Rocky group then sings the second stanza while waving Suzy's flashcard. The Grandad group replies with the second chorus.
Finally, read the words on the right-hand side of the page, asking pupils to repeat them. Then say the words at random and ask pupils to point to the words as they hear them.

Round-up

Activity Book (p. 12)

Draw, trace and say.
Pupils draw a self-portrait and practise the new vocabulary.

Focus pupils' attention on the page and ask them to identify the three characters. Elicit: Rocky – grandma – grandpa. Explain that these words are very common synonims for granny and grandad. Explain that Rocky wants to introduce his new friend to his grandparents. Point to the blank oval and ask them to draw and colour their faces inside it.
When they have finished, they show their self-portrait to their classmates. Finally, they trace the words at the bottom of the page.

Reinforcement activity: Play 'Sequences' using the family flashcards. (Resource File, Flashcards game 7, p. 79)

Extension activity: Pupils draw one grandparent and identify him/her by writing: My grandad (Pablo); My granny (Maria). Collect the drawings and make a display. When you take down the display, help pupils store their drawings in their Language Portfolio.

LESSON 4
Hello, friends! (p. 2)

Objectives: Sing the song and act it out. Reinforce the vocabulary of the unit. Identify different characters. Develop observation and fine motor skills.
Language focus: This is (Freddy). Freddy is my friend.
Vocabulary (revision): Dad, Mum, brother, sister, granny, grandad, friend, hello.
Materials: Unit flashcards. Class CD. Slips of paper (extension activity).

Warm-up
Revise the song on page 14.

Begin the lesson by singing and acting out the song on page 14. Play the CD. Encourage pupils to wave when they sing the word hello.

Preparing for the 'Join and say' activity
Revise the unit vocabulary.

Show the unit flashcards one by one and elicit the words. Draw a simple family tree on the board and hand out the flashcards to six pupils. Invite them to come to the board and stick their flashcard in the appropriate segment of the tree. The rest of the class then says the word.

Join and say. (p. 15)
Developing observation and fine motor skills.

Focus attention on the page. Point to Rocky, Suzy and Freddy and elicit their names.
Point to Rocky and trace the line joining him to his grandad with your finger. Explain to pupils that they are going to join the three characters to their grandparents.
Pupils observe each face carefully in order to find Rocky's granny, then draw a line joining Rocky to her. They do the same with Suzy and Freddy.
While pupils are working, go round the class and ask individual pupils to identify the characters and their grandparents.
Check the task by showing pupils a completed page.

Round-up

Check the unit vocabulary.

Write the unit vocabulary on the board, leaving out all the vowels. Pupils check the correct spelling in their Pupil's Book and complete the words in their notebooks.

Reinforcement activity: Play 'Red Rover' with the unit flashcards (Resource File, Flashcards game 9, p. 79).

Extension activity: Hand out a slip of paper to each pupil and tell them to write the name of a family member on it. Collect the slips and pick one at random. Read the name, for example: Lilian. Encourage the pupil who wrote it to stand and say: Lilian is my (sister). Do the same with all the slips.

LESSON 5
Let's listen! (p. 16)

> **Objectives:** Associate spoken words with pictures. Develop observation skills.
> Revise vocabulary. Develop awareness of appropriate behaviour when moving around in the classroom or at home.
> **Language focus:** Sh, sh, be quiet! (Granny)'s sleeping! Watch out! Ouch!
> Sorry, (granny)! Be careful! Look where you're going!
> **Vocabulary (revision):** granny, grandad, table, chair, door, window, bed, red, yellow, blue, green.
> **Materials:** Unit 2 flashcards. Flashcards of the characters and the colours. Class CD. Sheets of paper (extension activity).

Warm-up
Revise the unit vocabulary.

Show pupils the family flashcards and elicit the words. Then stick them on different walls and play 'Twist around.' (Resource File, TPR game 5, p. 77)

Pre-listening activity
Present the word 'sleeping'.

Pupils' books closed. Mime the verb 'sleeping' by leaning your head on your jointed hands. Close your eyes and say softly: Sleeping … I'm sleeping. Invite pupils to do the same while repeating the words. Then point to a pupil and say: Sh, sh, be quiet! (Mario)'s sleeping. Do this with several pupils.

🎧 **Let's listen! (p. 16)**
Present the vocabulary in context.

Focus pupils' attention on the scene. In L1, ask them to describe what is happening in the frames: Freddy, Suzy and Rocky are in the house. Granny is sleeping and Rocky has an accident.
Tell pupils to point to the table, the window and the chair.

2 My family

Present the comic using the CD and your book. Say: Listen and look at the pictures!

Audio script

1 ROCKY   Sh, sh, be quiet! Granny's sleeping!

2 ROCKY   Sh, sh, be quiet!

3 ROCKY   Grandad's sleeping!
  SUZY   Watch out, Rocky! Watch out!

4 ROCKY   Ouch, ouch!

5 ROCKY   Sorry, grandad! Sorry, granny!

6 ROCKY   Be careful! Look where you're going!

Make sure that pupils understand the dialogues. Then play the comic again, doing one of the following activities each time: **1** Pupils follow the comic in their books, pointing to each frame in turn. Say: Listen and point. **2** Pupils put their finger on their lips when they hear the words: Sh, sh, be quiet! They hold their heads when they hear the exclamation: Ouch, ouch! Say: Listen and do! **3** Play the CD again with pauses for them to repeat, chorally or individually. Check their pronunciation and intonation.

Round-up

Pupils act out the comic.

Divide the class into two groups and assign the roles of Rocky and Suzy. Give each group the flashcard of the corresponding character.
Play the CD again, with pauses after each line so that the groups can repeat it and mime the actions. Then swap roles and repeat the activity.

Reinforcement activity: Read out different lines from the comic and elicit the character's name each time.

Extension activity: Ask pupils to draw an accident that could happen if they don't look where they're going. Write on the board: Look where you're going! Pupils copy the sentence at the top of their pictures. Collect the drawings and make a display. When you take

down the display, help pupils store their drawings in their Language Portfolio.

LESSON 6
Let's play Bingo! (p. 17)

> **Objectives:** Revise and consolidate the vocabulary of the unit. Develop spoken interaction. Develop fine motor skills. Develop pre-reading, observation and memory skills.
> **Vocabulary (revision):** Mum, Dad, brother, sister, granny, grandad, window, door, bed, table, chair, pencil, crayon, book. Colours.
> **Materials:** Unit flashcards. Flashcards of Unit 1. Stickers. Nine tokens (or scraps of paper) per pupil to play Bingo. Formative assessment sheet (Resource File, p. 99). Sheets of paper (extension activity).

Warm-up
Revise the unit vocabulary.

Show the unit flashcards one by one and elicit the words as you stick them on the left-hand side of the board. Do the same with the flashcards of unit 1 and stick them on the right-hand side.
Say: Mum – book. Mum's got a book. Take both flashcards and stick them together. Stick the character first and then the object. Repeat: Mum's got a book. Give more examples with the rest of the flashcards. Pupils repeat chorally or individually.
Put the flashcards back in their original positions. Call different pupils to the board and say, for example: Grandad's got a chair. The pupil selects the appropriate flashcards and sticks them together. Encourage him/her to say the words. Repeat the procedure several times with different pupils.

Preparing for the Bingo! (p. 17 and stickers)
Pupils complete the family tree with stickers.

Focus pupils' attention on the page and ask pupils to identify Freddy's family. Tell them that they are going to play Bingo after covering the white circles with the

appropriate stickers.
Pupils go to the stickers page and look for the grandad sticker. When they find it, they peel it off, go back to page 17 and stick it in the appropriate circle. Do the same with the stickers of mum and brother.

Let's play Bingo! (p. 17)
Revise the unit vocabulary.

Focus pupils' attention on the page. Can they see Freddy and his friends there? Ask them to point to the characters as you name them. Then point to the different family members and ask: Who's this? Elicit the answers. Pupils repeat chorally or individually.
In L1, check they know how to play Bingo! Hand out nine tokens to each pupil. Say the words at random slowly, twice, for example: A yellow door. When the game is over, play again, asking a pupil to help you.

Round-up
Developing spoken interaction.

Pupils play in pairs. One says the words and the other covers them. Then they swap roles. Go round the room in order to give any necessary help and/or assess speaking skills using the Formative assessment sheet.

Reinforcement activity: Play 'Odd one out' with the flashcards of units 0, 1 and 2 (Resource File, Flashcards game 8, p. 79).

Extension activity: Hand out the sheets of paper, one per pupil. Show the class how to fold them three times to make six squares. Pupils make up their own Bingo game using colours, classroom objects and family members. Play with the class, holding up the flashcard of the word you are calling.

LESSON 7
Colour, stick and say.
Activity Book (p. 13)

Objectives: Develop fine motor skills. Revise the unit vocabulary. Develop spoken interaction.
Language focus : Is it (dad)?
Vocabulary (revision): Mum, Dad, brother, sister, granny, grandad, window. Colours.
Materials: Unit flashcards. Photocopies of Cut-Out (p. 101). Your completed page 3 from the Activity book. Formative assessment sheet (Resource File, p. 99).

Warm-up
Revise the unit vocabulary and the song on page 14.

Begin the lesson by singing and acting out the unit song (p. 14). Play the CD and encourage everyone to join in.

Colour, stick and say.
Developing spoken interaction.

Focus pupils' attention on the page. Say: This is a house. Point to the window and ask: What's this? Elicit: A window. Ask them how many windows there are. Explain that they are going to complete the page by sticking blinds on the windows. Show them your finished page.
Hand out the photocopies of page 101 (Resource File). Ask them to cut out the blinds and colour them using a colour that they know in English. Show them how to fold the flaps before sticking them on the page. Pupils then go back to page 13.

Guessing game
Developing spoken interaction.

Play the following guessing game with different pupils. Point to a blind on the page and ask: Is it (dad)? Elicit: Yes or No.
Pupils play in pairs. To make the game more challenging, they can turn their books sideways or upside down. Go round the room to help them and/or assess speaking skills using the Formative assessment sheet.

2 My family

Round-up

Display the pupils' finished pages.

Prepare a display of the Activity Book pages so that pupils can see their classmates' work.

8 Reinforcement activity: Pupils repeat the chant from lesson 1 while pointing to Suzy's family on the page.

Extension activity: Play 'Pass the flashcards' using the unit flashcards (Resource File, Flashcards game 6, p. 79).

LESSON 8
My world! (p. 18)

Objectives: Associate spoken words with pictures. Develop listening comprehension skills. Revise vocabulary. Transfer the new language into an authentic context.
Language focus: This is my family. My granny, my grandad, my mum, my dad, my sister and me!
Vocabulary (revision): Vocabulary of Unit 2. Colours.
Materials: Unit flashcards. Colour and characters' flashcards. Class CD.

Warm-up
Revise the vocabulary of units 0-2.

Hand out the unit and colour flashcards to different pupils and elicit the words. Say: Blue – mum. Pupils holding the flashcards stand up and show them to the class. To make the activity more fun, vary the rhythm of the instructions. If you speak slowly, pupils show the flashcards slowly, and vice versa.

12 Listen and point. (p. 18)
Developing listening comprehension.

Focus pupils' attention on the page. Point to the boy and say: Look, this is his family! Ask pupils to point to the

appropriate persons as you name them. Say: Point to (granny).
Read the words in the boxes while pupils point to the persons. Then reverse the activity by calling out the names while pupils point to the words.
Next point to Rocky's family and play 'Touch red.' (Resource File, TPR game 1, p. 77)
Finally invite pupils to listen to the child speaking about his family. Play Track 12.

Audio script

BOY This is my family!
My mum, my dad, my granny,
my grandad, my sister and me!

Play the CD again, doing one of the following activities each time: **1** Pupils listen and point to the family members in their books as they hear the words. Say: Listen and point. **2** Play the CD again with pauses for them to repeat, chorally or individually. Check their pronunciation and intonation.

Draw, colour and say.
Developing observation skills and revising colours.

Ask pupils to take out their pencils and crayons. Explain the task: they are going to complete the second half of each drawing by focusing on the empty squares on the right-hand side and observing the mirror image on the left in order to draw in the missing lines correctly. When they finish, they colour the drawing.
Go round the room to help pupils with the activity. Ask individual pupils to identify the colours they use.

Reinforcement activity: Pupils go to page 18 of the Pupil's Book and in pairs, give each other instructions such as: Touch granny! Touch brother!

Extension activity: Help pupils create a display with photos of human and animal families. These can be cut out of magazines and mounted on poster paper. Write 'Families' as the poster title. Then ask different pupils to point to a family on the poster and identify the members of the family they can name in English. Help them say for example: This is dad. This is granny. etc.

LESSON 9
My turn! (p. 19)

Objectives: Revise and consolidate the vocabulary and structures of Unit 2. Revise the unit song. Develop listening skills. Develop pre-reading and pre-writing skills. To do assessment and self-assessment activities.
Language (revision): Structures of the unit.
Vocabulary (revision): Unit vocabulary.
Materials: Tokens or scraps of paper (five per child). Class CD. Unit flashcards.

Warm-up
Revise the unit song and vocabulary.

Begin the lesson by singing and acting out the unit song (p. 14). Encourage everyone to join in.

My turn! (p. 19)
Pupils give personal information using the language learnt.

Focus pupils' attention on the page. Point to the words at the bottom and read them. Pupils point to the words as they hear them.
Stick the unit flashcards on the board one by one. Elicit each word, then write it under the corresponding flashcard. Then play 'Words and pictures' (Resource File, Flashcards game 13, p. 80). Leave the flashcards on the board for the next activity.
Focus pupils' attention on the frame. Ask them to draw and colour a family there (their own, an imaginary family, an animal family, etc.). When they have finished, they label their picture using the words at the bottom of the page.
Go round the room to help pupils with the activity.
Ask individual pupils to identify the members of the family.

Round-up

Activity Book (p. 15)

Listen and find.
Developing listening skills and identifying family members.

Focus pupils attention on the page and explain the task. Pupils have to cover a face in each row with a token or a scrap of paper according to your instructions.
Hand out five tokens to each pupil. Point to the first row and say: This is (sister). Repeat twice.
Do the same with the other rows.
Check the task by asking different pupils to identify the faces they have covered.

End-of-unit sticker
Focus pupils' attention on the empty circle on the right-hand corner of the frame on page 19. Tell pupils that Rocky is happy because they have finished Unit 2 and ask them to peel off Rocky's sticker in the middle of the book and complete the page.

Reinforcement activity: Repeat the activity on page 15 (Activity Book) using different words.

Extension activity: Pupils work in pairs. One pupil says the words and the other covers them. Then they swap roles.

Picture dictionary
Turn to page 41 and tell pupils they are going to revise the unit vocabulary orally and in writing. Point to the pictures in the order they are presented and ask pupils to identify them. Then point to the pictures at random and do the same. Finally, pupils trace over the words.

Testing and Assessment

Unit test
Photocopy Test 2 on pages 89 and 90 and hand out one copy to each pupil. Pupils complete the test individually. Once you have corrected all the tests, return them to pupils and help them check their performance by writing the answers on the board. Record pupils' results on the End of unit assessment sheet (Resource File, p. 100). Make sure they file their tests in their Language Portfolio.

If you need to consolidate or develop the unit further, please turn to the Resource File (p. 77).

Unit 3 Food

Food (pp. 20-21)

Objectives: Recognise and name some food items. Develop fine motor skills. Reinforce colours and counting.
Language focus: I like (apples).
Target vocabulary: apple, banana, orange, biscuit, four, five.
Vocabulary (revision): red, yellow. Numbers from 1 to 3.
Materials: Flashcards (apple, banana, orange and biscuit). Class CD. Realia: a banana, an apple, an orange and a plain biscuit (extension activity).

Warm-up
Revising colours.

Play 'Touch red' (Resource File, TPR game 1, p. 77). Read and explain the title of the unit. In L1, ask pupils to name some of their favourite foods.

Pre-listening activities (pp. 20-21)
Present food items.

Pupils' books closed. Stick the flashcards of the fruits on the board one by one. Say: Look, this is a (banana). Encourage pupils to repeat chorally or individually. Remove the flashcards from the board and stick them on different walls. Pupils point to the items you indicate. Say: Point to (the apple)! Repeat several times, increasing the speed and varying the order of the instructions.

Pupils' books open. Focus pupils' attention on the scene. Point to the characters and say: Look! This is … Elicit: Rocky. In L1 explain that he is at the market with Suzy and Freddy. Point to Freddy and ask what he is doing.
Pupils observe the scene and try to predict what Freddy is trying to pick up. Confirm that it is a box of biscuits.

Show them the sticker in the middle of the book and ask them to peel it off. Then, they go back to page 21 and, once they are sure of the position, they stick it on the page.

1 **Let's chant. (pp. 20-21)**
Pupils practise the pronunciation of the new vocabulary.

Pupils' books open. Focus pupils' attention on the scene and describe the situation: Rocky and Suzy are pointing to some fruits and Freddy is trying to pick up a packet of biscuits.
Point to the fruit and elicit the words: Bananas, apples, oranges. Elicit the colours: Bananas – yellow. Apples – red. Then present the word orange: fruit and colour. Pupils repeat chorally an individually.
Present the chant with the CD and the book.
Encourage pupils to listen and look at you while you point in your book. Say: Listen!

Audio script

ROCKY   Apples, apples,
         I like apples!

         Oranges, oranges,
         I like oranges!

         Bananas, bananas,
         I like bananas!

FREDDY   Biscuits, biscuits,
         I like biscuits!

Play the chant again, doing one of the following activities each time: **1** Pupils point to the food items in their books. Say: Listen and point. **2** Ask pupils to choose their favourite food item on the page and tell them to stand up when they hear it. **3** Pause after each verse and encourage pupils to repeat. Say: Listen and repeat!

Round-up

Activity Book (p. 6)

Count and say.
Counting food items.

Begin by counting on your fingers slowly. Say: One, two, three, four, five. Encourage pupils to do the same. Then invite them to count up to 5 tables and chairs in the room.

Pupils go to page 16 of the Activity Book. In L1, explain that they are going to count some food items.

Point to the fruit items at the bottom of the page and elicit them. Ask: What's this? Elicit: An apple. Do the same with the banana and the orange. Explain that they have to count the apples, the oranges and the bananas, and write the number in the corresponding box.

Go round the room to help pupils with the activity. Check by naming each item and eliciting the corresponding number. Say: Bananas and elicit: Five. Do the same with the oranges and the apples. Then do the opposite: say the number first and elicit the type of fruit then.

Reinforcement activity: Play 'What is it?' using the flashcards. (Resource File, Flashcard game 5, p. 79)

Extension activity: Put an apple, an orange, a banana and a plain biscuit in a bag. Ask different pupils to close their eyes, touch one of the items and guess what it is. They say the word and show it to the class. Encourage them to say: This is (a banana).

LESSON 2
Food (pp. 20-21)

Objectives: Reinforce food items. Develop fine motor skills. Develop pre-reading and pre-writing skills. Solve a puzzle.
Language focus: I like (apples).
Vocabulary (revision): Orange, apple, banana, biscuit, mum, dad, brother, sister. Colours.
Materials: Flashcards (apple, banana, orange and biscuit). Red, yellow and orange crayons. Class CD. Family flashcards (extension activity).

13 Warm-up
Revise the chant.

Begin the lesson by chanting and acting out the unit chant. Play the CD and encourage everyone to join in.

Pupils' books open. Focus pupils' attention on the double spread. Play the CD again, asking them to follow the chant and point to the food items as they hear them.

2 14 Listen, join and colour. (p. 21)
Developing listening skills and practising the new vocabulary.

Read the words and ask pupils to repeat them. Ask pupils to take out red, yellow and orange crayons. Hold them up one by one and elicit the colours:
This is … (orange).
Pupils follow your instructions. Say: Show me red … yellow … orange. Do this several times, varying the order and the rhythm.
Pupils listen to Track 14 and join each pencil to the corresponding piece of fruit. They mark each fruit item with a dot of colour and finish colouring them once the listening activity is finished.

Audio script

Yellow – banana
The banana is yellow.
Orange – orange
The orange is orange.

Red – apple
The apple is red.

Go round the room to help pupils with the activity. Check by naming each item and eliciting the colour. Say: Banana and elicit: Yellow. Do the same with the orange and the apple. Then repeat the procedure, saying the colour first, and then the corresponding item.

Round-up

Activity Book (p. 17)

Trace, find and colour.
Developing observation and pre-writing skills.

Point to the food items and elicit the words. Focus attention on the written words and ask pupils to trace them.
In L1, ask pupils to find the food items in the grid and colour them in according to the models.
Go round the room to help pupils with the activity. Ask individual pupils to identify the items and their colour.

Reinforcement activity: Play 'Pass it on' with the unit flashcards (Resource File, TPR game 3, p. 77).

Extension activity: Play 'Guess the flashcard' using the family and food flashcards (Resource File, Flashcards game 12, p. 79).

LESSON 3

Let's sing and do! (p. 22)

Objectives: Present the word '(glass of) milk' and reinforce the word 'biscuit.' Develop listening comprehension skills. Develop pre-reading and pre-writing skills. Sing a song and act it out.
Language focus: I'm hungry! Can I have a snack, please? Here's a biscuit!
Target vocabulary: A glass of milk.
Vocabulary (revision): biscuit, orange, banana, apple. Counting from 1 to 5.
Materials: Flashcards (apple, banana, orange, biscuit and milk). Class CD. One sheet of paper per pupil (reinforcement activity).

Warm up
Present 'I'm hungry' and 'milk.'

Stick the unit flashcards on the board one by one. Elicit the words: Apple, orange, biscuit, banana. Introduce the word 'milk' showing the appropriate flashcard. Pupils repeat the words chorally and individually. Rub your stomach and say: I'm hungry! Repeat it several times and encourage pupils to do the same. Point to the apple and say: I'm hungry! Mmmmm! An apple! Pupils repeat chorally and individually. Do the same with the orange, the banana and the biscuit.

Pre-listening activity
Preparing for the song.

Pupils' books closed. Hand out the flashcards of the unit to different pupils. Point to one pupil and say: Can I have a snack, please? Encourage the pupil to answer: Here's a (banana)! Repeat this several times. When you finish, pupils pass their flashcards on to their partners and repeat the procedure.

1 15 **Let's sing and do! (p. 22)**
Practising the pronunciation of the new words and memorise them through gestures.

Pupils' books open. Focus pupils' attention on page 22. Tell them to point to the food items as you name

them. Say: Point to the (orange)!
Present the song using the CD and the book. Pupils listen and look at the pictures as you point to them in your book. Say: Listen to the song!

Audio script

BOY Mum, Mum,
      I'm hungry,
      Can I have a snack,
      Please?

MUM Here's an orange,
      Here's a biscuit,
      Here's a glass of milk,
      Just for you!

BOY An orange,
      A biscuit,
      A glass of milk,
      Just for me!

Play the song again doing one of the following activities each time: **1** Pupils listen to the song and point to each food in their books. Say: Listen and point. **2** Stick the flashcards of the orange, the milk and the biscuit on different walls. Pupils do the actions with you, pointing to the flashcards. Say: Listen and do! **3** Pupils do the actions and sing along. Say: Sing and do! **4** Divide the class into two groups and assign the roles (the mum and the boy). Each group sings and acts out their part while the other claps hands to the rhythm.
Finally, read the words at the bottom of the page, asking pupils to repeat them. Then repeat the words at random and ask pupils to point to the words as they hear them.

Round-up

Activity Book (p. 18)

Find the 4 differences. Draw and say.
Developing observation skills and reinforcing the vocabulary (numbers and food).

Focus pupils' attention on the first picture, point to the biscuits and say: Let's count the biscuits! One, two, three, four, five biscuits. Then focus their attention on the biscuits in the second picture and do the same: One, two, three, four biscuits. Explain in L1 that they have to draw one biscuit in order to have 5 biscuits in both pictures.
They compare the pictures and do the same with the remaining food items.
Check orally with the whole class.

Reinforcement activity: Hand out a sheet of paper to each pupil. Ask them to draw an orange, a biscuit and a glass of milk large enough to cut out. Play the song again (Track 15). Pupils do the actions with you, raising their drawings when they hear the word. Say: Listen and do!

Extension activity: Play 'Chinese Whispers' using the unit flashcards (Resource File, Flashcards game 1, p. 78).

LESSON 4
Join and say. (p. 23)

Objectives: Sing the song and act it out. Reinforce the unit vocabulary. Do a maze.
Language focus: I'm hungry! Can I have a snack, please? Here's a biscuit!
Vocabulary (revision): biscuit, orange, banana, apple, milk, brother, sister, mum, dad, granny, grandad. Colours.
Materials: Flashcards (apple, banana, orange, milk and family). Class CD. Orange, red and yellow crayons. Realia: an apple, a banana, an orange, a biscuit and a small carton of milk.

Warm-up
Revise the unit song.

Stick the flashcards of the orange, the biscuit and the milk on different walls. Begin the lesson by singing and acting out the song (p. 22). Play the CD.

3 Food

Encourage pupils to join in and do the actions pointing to the flashcards as they hear the words.
Play 'Twist around' using the unit flashcards (Resource File, TPR game 5, p. 77).

Preparing for the 'Join and say' activity.
Revise family members and food items.

Draw a large three-level tree on the board with two branches on each level. Stick the flashcards of the family on the branches: granny and grandad at the top, mum and dad on the second level and brother and sister on the third. Point to each flashcard and say the corresponding word. Encourage pupils to repeat chorally and individually. Then point to the flashcards at random and elicit the words.

Join and say. (p. 23)
Pupils do the maze.

Pupils take out orange, red and yellow crayons. Ask them to hold up the appropriate crayon when you say: Show me (orange).
Focus pupils' attention on the page. Point to the characters on the left and say: sister, mum, brother. In L1, explain that they are hungry and need help in order to reach their snacks.
Point to the girl and say: Sister! Follow the path with your finger down to the milk and orange on the right. Say: Sister – milk and orange.
Pupils then trace the path from the sister to the milk and orange with a red crayon. When they finish ask them to do the same with the other characters using a yellow crayon for the mum and an orange one for the brother.
While pupils are working, go round the class and ask individual pupils to identify the characters and their snacks.
Check with the whole class by pointing and saying: Sister… red. Help pupils reply: Milk and orange. Do the same with the other characters.

Round-up
Check the unit vocabulary.

Play 'In the bag' using real food items (Resource File, TPR game 6, p. 78).

Reinforcement activity: Play 'Let's dance' with the flashcards of the unit (Resource File, TPR game 8, p. 78).

Extension activity: Play 'Vanishing pictures' using the flashcards of the unit (Resource File, Flashcards game 11, p. 79)

LESSON 5
Let's listen! (p. 24)

Objectives: Associate spoken words with pictures. Develop observation skills. Revise vocabulary. Develop healthy eating habits.
Language focus: I like lunch! Lunch is ready! Can I have an (apple), please?
Target vocabulary: chicken, ice cream, chocolate.
Vocabulary (revision): apple, banana, orange, biscuit.
Materials: Unit flashcards. Class CD. Sheets of paper (extension activity).

Warm-up
Revise the unit vocabulary.

Play the 'Echo Game' using the flashcards of the unit (Resource File, Flashcards game 2, p. 78).

Pre-listening activity
Present the words 'chicken', 'ice cream' and 'chocolate'.

Pupils' books closed. Present chicken, ice cream and chocolate with the help of the flashcards. Stick them on the board. Point to each flashcard and say the appropriate word. Pupils repeat chorally and individually. Then point to the food items at random and elicit the words.
Play 'Twist around' using the complete set of unit flashcards (Resource File, TPR game 5, p. 77).

Let's listen! (p. 24)
Present the new words in context.

Focus pupils' attention on the comic. In L1, ask them to

describe what is happening in the frames: Freddy is busy in the kitchen. Suzy, Rocky and a friend arrive for lunch. Suzy is not happy with the food.
Tell pupils to point to the chicken, the ice cream, the chocolate, the banana and the apple. Say: Point to the (chocolate)!
Present the comic using the CD and your book. Say: Listen and look at the pictures!

Audio script

1 FREDDY Chicken, chicken, I like chicken!

2 FREDDY Chocolate, chocolate, I like chocolate!

3 FREDDY Ice cream, ice cream, I like ice cream!

4 FREDDY I'm coming!!! Hello friends!

5 FREDDY Lunch is ready – look! Ice cream, chocolate and chicken!
   SUZY   Oh, no! Can I have an apple, please?

6 SUZY   Eat vegetables and fruit every day!

Make sure that pupils understand the dialogues. Then play the comic again, doing one of the following activities each time: **1** Pupils follow the comic in their books, pointing to each frame as they hear the corresponding dialogue. Say: Listen and point. **2** Stick the flashcards of the chocolate, ice cream and chicken on different walls. Pupils point to the flashcards when they hear the words. Say: Listen and do! **3** Play the CD again with pauses for them to repeat chorally or individually. Check their pronunciation and intonation.

Round-up

Pupils act out the comic.

Divide the class into two groups and assign the roles of Freddy and Suzy. Give each group the flashcard of one character.
Play the CD again, pausing after each line so the groups can repeat it and mime the actions. If you have time, swap roles and repeat the activity.

Reinforcement activity: Read out different lines from the comic and elicit the character's name each time.

Extension activity: Ask pupils to draw the fruits and vegetables they like best. On the board, write: Eat vegetables and fruit every day! Pupils copy the sentence at the top of their pictures. Collect the drawings and display them. After some time, take them down and make sure that pupils store their drawings in their Language Portfolio.

LESSON 6
Let's play Bingo! (p. 25)

Objectives: Revise and consolidate the vocabulary of the unit. Develop spoken interaction. Develop fine motor skills. Develop pre-reading, observation and memory skills.
Language focus: What's this?
Vocabulary (revision): Biscuit, milk, apple, orange, banana, chicken, ice cream, chocolate.
Materials: Unit flashcards. Stickers. Eight tokens (or scraps of paper) per pupil to play Bingo. Formative assessment sheet (Resource File, p. 99).

Warm-up
Revise the unit vocabulary.

Show the unit flashcards one by one and elicit the words. Then play 'Sequences' (Resource File, Flashcards game 7, p. 79).

Preparing for the Bingo! (p. 25 and stickers)
Pupils complete the drawing with the stickers.

Focus pupils' attention on the page. Tell pupils that they are going to play Bingo but have to complete the drawing with the stickers, first. Pupils predict what food items are missing (milk, chicken and ice cream). Pupils go to the stickers page and look for the milk sticker. When they find it, they remove it and go back to page 25. Ask them to stick it in any of the white circles. Do the same with the stickers of the chicken and the ice cream.

Let's play Bingo! (p. 25)
Checking comprehension of the unit vocabulary.

Focus pupils' attention on the page. Ask them to identify some of the food items. Point and ask: What's this? Elicit: An (apple).
In L1, remind them of how to play Bingo! Hand out eight tokens to each pupil. Say the words at random slowly twice, for example: Ice cream. When the game is over, play again asking a pupil to help you.

Round-up
Developing spoken interaction.

Pupils play in pairs. One says the words and the other covers them. Then they swap roles. Go round the room and help them if necessary. Now you can assess speaking skills using the Formative assessment sheet.

Reinforcement activity: Play the 'Echo Game' with the unit flashcards (Resource File, Flashcards game 2, p. 78).

Extension activity: Give pupils a few moments to memorise the items on page 25. Tell them to remember where each food item is. Pupils' books closed, ask: First column? Elicit: Three biscuits, an apple, a banana… (The last item depends on the sticker that pupil chose). Do the same with the second column. Pupils check the answers by looking at the page.

LESSON 7
Trace, stick and say.
Activity Book (p. 19)

Objectives: Develop fine motor skills. Revise the unit vocabulary. Develop pre-reading and pre-writing skills.
Language focus: What's this?
Vocabulary (revision): chicken, chocolate, milk, ice cream, biscuit, banana, apple, orange.
Materials: Unit flashcards. Photocopies of page 102, Resource File (one per pupil). A completed page 19 (AB).

Warm-up
Revise the song on page 22.

Stick the flashcards of the orange, biscuit and milk on different walls. Begin the lesson by singing and acting out the unit song (p. 22). Play the CD. Encourage pupils to join and point to the flashcards as they hear the words.

Trace, stick and say.
Developing pre-reading and pre-writing skills.

Pupils' books closed. Play 'Words and pictures' (Resource File, Flashcards game 13, p. 80).

Pupils' books open. Focus pupils' attention on the page. Say: Look, this is Rocky. He wants his lunch! Tell pupils that they are going to find out what Rocky is going to eat by tracing the words and sticking the food items in the appropriate circles. Show them your finished page.
Hand out the photocopies of the cut-outs on page 102. Point to the chicken and tell them to colour it in and cut it out.
Pupils go back to page 19. Show them how to trace the word chicken and stick the picture on the word of the AB page. Follow the same procedure with the rest of the food items.
Go round the room to help pupils if necessary and ask individual pupils to identify the food items.

Guessing game
Developing spoken interaction.

Play the following guessing game with different pupils: ask them to cover two food items with a scrap of paper. Then try to guess what they have chosen by asking questions. Ask: Is it the (chicken)? Elicit: Yes or No. Repeat this several times.
Pupils play in pairs. Go round the room in order to help them and/or assess their speaking skills using the Formative assessment sheet.

Round-up
Display the pupils' finished pages.

Display of Activity Book pages so that pupils can see their classmates' work.

Reinforcement activity: Play 'Pass it on' (Resource File, TPR game 3, p. 77).

Extension activity: Make a chart by drawing five columns with the following headings on the board: chicken / ice cream / chocolate / milk / biscuit. Tell pupils that they are going to complete a survey by choosing their favourite food item from the chart. Record their answers on the chart. Name a pupil and ask: Rosa, what's your favourite food? Put a tick under the pupil's choice. Follow the same procedure with the rest of the pupils. Encourage them to ask their classmates with you. Finally count the ticks and state the results: (Chocolate) is the most popular favourite food.

LESSON 8
My world! (p. 26)

Objectives: Associate spoken words with pictures. Develop listening comprehension skills. Revise vocabulary. Transfer the new language into an authentic context.
Language focus: What's for lunch? Fruit and vegetables.
Vocabulary (revision): Chicken, chocolate, milk, ice cream, biscuit, banana, apple, orange.
Materials: Unit flashcards. Flashcards of the family. Class CD. Magazine cut-outs of real foods. Poster paper.

Warm-up
Revise the vocabulary presented so far.

Show the unit and family flashcards one by one. Elicit the words as you stick the food items on one side of the board and the family members on the other.
Call a pupil to the board and say: Mum likes chicken and milk. The pupil points to the appropriate flashcards. Do this with several pupils. Finally invite some pupils to say the sentences for their classmates.

Listen and point. (p. 26)
Develop listening comprehension skills.

Focus pupils' attention on the page. Point to Freddy and say: Look, Freddy is in a restaurant! Ask pupils to point to the food items as you name them. Say: Point to the (chicken).
Present the words vegetables and fruit by pointing to the appropriate platters. Pupils repeat the words chorally and individually.
Finally, invite pupils to listen to Freddy speaking about lunch. Play the CD.

Audio script

FREDDY   What's for lunch today? Chicken, vegetables, fruit and milk. Oh, yummy!

Play the CD again doing one of the following activities each time: **1** Pupils follow the listening in their books,

Food

pointing to the food items as they hear the words. Say: Listen and point. **2** Play the CD again with pauses for them to repeat chorally or individually. Check their pronunciation and intonation.

Round-up

Activity Book (p. 20)

Draw, colour and say.
Developing observation skills and revising colours.

Ask pupils to take out their crayons. Say: Show me green … yellow … blue, etc.
Explain the task: they are going to complete the second half of each drawing by focusing on the empty squares on the right-hand side and observing the mirror image on the left in order to draw in the missing lines correctly. When they finish, they colour the drawing.
Go round the room to help pupils if necessary. Ask individual pupils to identify the items and the colours.

Reinforcement activity: Play 'Guess the flashcard' with the unit and family flashcards (Resource File, Flashcards game 12, p. 79).

Extension activity: Help pupils create a display with photos of real foods. These can be cut out of magazines and mounted on poster paper. Write 'Foods' as the poster title. Then ask different pupils to point to the poster and identify food items they can say in English. Help them to say for example: This is a (banana).

LESSON 9
My turn! (p. 27)

Objectives: Revise and consolidate the vocabulary and structures of Unit 3. Revise the unit song. Develop listening skills. Develop pre-reading and pre-writing skills. Do assessment and self-assessment activities.
Language (revision): Structures of the unit.
Vocabulary (revision): Unit vocabulary.
Materials: Five tokens or scraps of paper per child. Class CD. Unit flashcards.

Warm-up
Revise the unit song and vocabulary.

Stick the flashcards of the orange, biscuit and milk on different walls. Begin the lesson by singing and acting out the unit song (p. 22). Play the CD. Encourage everyone to join in and do the actions pointing to the flashcards as they hear the words.
Play 'Twist around' with the class using the unit flashcards (Resource File, TPR game 5, p. 77).

My turn! (p. 27)
Pupils give personal information using the language learnt.

Focus pupils' attention on the page. Point to the words at the bottom and read them. Pupils point to the words as they hear them.
Stick the unit flashcards on the board one by one. Elicit each word, then write it under the corresponding flashcard. Then play 'Words and pictures' with the class (Resource File, game 13, p. 80) Leave the flashcards on the board for the next activity.
Focus pupils' attention on the tray. Ask pupils to draw and colour four food items that they like and have learnt in the unit. When they finish, they label their pictures.
Go round the room in order to help pupils with the activity. Ask individual pupils to identify the food items. Help them say: I like (chocolate and bananas).

Round-up

Activity Book (p. 21)

Listen and find.
Developing listening skills and identifying food items.

Focus pupils' attention on the page and explain the activity. Pupils have to put a token or a scrap of paper on one food item in each row according to your instructions.
Hand out five tokens to each pupil. Point to the first row and say: This is a biscuit. Repeat twice.
Do the same with the remaining rows, choosing one item each time.
Check the task by asking different pupils to identify the items they have covered.

End-of-unit sticker
Focus pupils' attention on the empty circle on the right-hand corner of the tray on page 27. Tell pupils that Rocky is happy because they have finished Unit 3 and ask them to peel off Rocky's sticker in the middle of the book and complete the page.

Reinforcement activity: Repeat the activity on page 21 (AB) using different words.

Extension activity: Pupils work in pairs. One pupil says the words and the other covers them. Then they swap roles.

Picture dictionary
Turn to page 42 and tell pupils they are going to revise the unit vocabulary orally and in writing. Point to the pictures in order and ask pupils to identify them. Then point to the pictures at random and do the same. Finally, pupils trace over the words.

Testing and Assessment

Unit test
Photocopy the Test 3 on pages 91 and 92 and hand out one copy to each pupil. Pupils complete the test individually. Once you have corrected all the tests, return them to the pupils and help them check their performance by writing the answers on the board. Record pupils' results on the End of unit assessment sheet (Resource File, p. 100). Make sure they file their tests in their Language Portfolio.

If you need to consolidate or develop the unit further, please turn to the Resource File (page 77).

I'M HUNGRY!

Pages 28-29

Objectives: Listening to a story in English for pleasure. Develop observation skills. Consolidate the vocabulary of units 1-3. Develop healthy eating habits.

Language focus: I'm hungry! Here's a (biscuit) for you! Oh thanks, (Jimmy)! Lunch is ready, Lucky. My favourite lunch! Thanks, Mum! I'm not hungry. Sorry, Mum. Don't nibble. Wait for lunch. Lunch is on the table.

Vocabulary (revision): Food, family and items of furniture.

Materials: Flashcards of units 1-3. Class CD.

Warm-up

Revise and consolidate vocabulary.

Take out the flashcards of units 1-3 and shuffle them. Tell pupils that you are going to check if they remember the vocabulary of the previous units. Choose 12 flashcards at random and place them face down on your desk.

Show the flashcards one by one and tell pupils to raise their hands if they know the word. Call on one pupil to say it aloud. If it is correct, write a tick on the board. If it is incorrect, ask another pupil. The activity ends when the pupils have identified all 12 flashcards and you have 12 ticks on the board.

1 Look and find. (p. 28)

Developing observation and pre-listening activities skills.

Pupils' books open. Focus pupils' attention on the comic. Read the title and explain that they are going to hear about a little boy who is hungry.

Point to the book, the chair and the table. Tell pupils that these objects are somewhere in the frames. Pupils observe the frames carefully in order to find the red book (frame 7), the yellow chair (frame 5) and the green table (frame 8).

2 18 Listen to the story and the song. (pp. 28-29)

Developing listening-comprehension skills and consolidating the language.

Focus pupils' attention on the story and ask them to describe what is going on: A little boy is playing in the park. Some friends give him things to eat, and then he goes home for lunch.

Ask: Where are the biscuits? (In frames 1 and 2.) Where are the bananas? (In frame 3 and 4.) Where is the chocolate? (In frames 5 and 6.)

Play the CD. Pupils listen and follow the story.

Audio script

1 LUCKY Hey, Jimmy, I'm hungry! I'm really hungry!

2 JIMMY Here's a biscuit for you!
   LUCKY Oh thanks, Jimmy!

3 LUCKY Hey, Jenny, I'm hungry! I'm really hungry!

4 JENNY Here's a banana for you!
   LUCKY Oh thanks, Jenny!

5 LUCKY Hey, Monty, I'm hungry! I'm really hungry!

6 MONTY Here's some chocolate for you!
   LUCKY Oh, thanks, Monty!

7 MUM Lunch is ready, Lucky.
   LUCKY My favourite lunch! Thanks, Mum!

8 LUCKY Oooh, I'm not hungry. Sorry, Mum, I'm not hungry!

Song

CHORUS If you are hungry,
        Don't nibble,
        Don't nibble,
        Wait for lunch,
        Please!

MUM   Lunch is on the table,
         Chicken, milk and fruit,
         Lunch is on the table,
         Lunch is waiting for you!

Ask pupils to explain why Lucky isn't hungry for lunch. Do they sometimes act like Lucky? Why is it not a good idea to nibble between meals?
Play the CD again, doing one of the following activities each time: **1** Pupils point to the frames in their books. Say: Listen and follow the story in your books! **2** Pause after each frame, encouraging pupils to repeat the dialogue. Say: Listen and say!

Round-up

Developing listening skills and checking comprehension.

Retell the story frame by frame, changing the following words:
Frame 2: say banana instead of biscuit. Frame 4, say apple instead of banana. Frame 6, say ice cream instead of chocolate. Frame 8, say I'm hungry instead of I'm not hungry.

Note: Turning the stories into one-act plays. Ideas in the Resource File, page 80.

My body

My body (pp. 30-31)

Objectives: Recognise and name parts of the body. Count to six. Develop fine motor skills.
Language focus: Move your (head). Stamp your feet.
Target vocabulary: head, arms, legs, feet, body, rabbit, pirate, one, two, three, four, five, six.
Materials: Photo of a male or female athlete. Flashcards of the head, arms, legs and feet. Class CD.

Warm-up

Introduce the new topic and some new words.

In L1, tell pupils that in this unit they are going to talk about their bodies.
Pin up the photo of the athlete you have brought. Point to his/her head and say: Head. It's his/her head. Point to the arms, legs and feet and present the words in the same way. Then point to the entire person and say: It's his/her body.

Pre-listening activities. (pp. 30-31)

Pupils familiarise with the new language and complete the scene with a sticker.

Pupils' books closed. Draw the outline of a body on the board. Point to the head and say: Head. Pupils repeat chorally and individually. Do the same with the arms, legs and feet.
Call different pupils to the board. Say: Point to the (head). Point to the (feet). Pupils do the same at their desks, pointing to their own body as they repeat the words. Do this several times, increasing the speed and varying the order of the instructions.

Pupils' books open. Focus pupils' attention on the scene. Point to the characters and elicit their names. Ask them to identify the last animal (a rabbit). In L1, ask what the characters are doing (exercising). Ask

pupils if they do their exercises every day.
Pupils observe the whole scene and try to predict what is missing. Point to the number board and say: One … Elicit: Two, three. Confirm that numbers 2, 3 and 6 are missing, then count right up to 6.
Show pupils the number stickers in the middle of the book. Ask them to peel them off and go back to page 30. Once they are sure of the position, they stick them on the pages.

1 **19** **Let's chant. (pp. 30-31)**
Pupils practise the pronunciation of the new words.

Pupils' books open. Focus pupils' attention on the complete scene and describe the situation: Rocky and his friends are doing their exercises.
Present the chant with the CD and the book.
Encourage pupils to listen and look at you while you point to Rocky, Suzy, Freddy and the rabbit. Say: Listen!

Audio script

One, two, three,
Head,
Move your head.
Arms,
Move your arms,

Head and arms,
One, two, three.

Four, five, six,
Legs,
Move your legs.
Feet,
Stamp your feet,

Head and arms,
Legs and feet,
One, two, three!
Four, five, six!

Play the chant again, doing one of the following activities each time: **1** Pupils point to the parts of the

body in their books. Say: Listen and point. **2** Pupils clap the appropriate number of times when they hear the numbers. Say: Listen and clap. **3** Pause after each verse and encourage pupils to repeat and do the actions. Say: Listen and repeat!

Round-up

Activity Book (p. 22)

Find and colour.
Developing observation and fine motor skills.

Pupils go to page 22 of the Activity Book. Point to the pirate and say: He's a pirate! Point to his head, arms, legs and foot and elicit the words. In L1, ask pupils to find him in the drawing and colour him according to the model.
Go round the room to help pupils if necessary. Ask individual pupils to identify the parts of the body. When they finish, show them the completed page so they can check their work.

Reinforcement activity: Hold up your book to the class. Say the chant and point to the pictures in turn. Repeat, this time inviting pupils to complete your sentences.
Example:
Teacher: One, two, three,
Pupils: Move your head!

Extension activity: In pairs, pupils give each other similar instructions using the lesson vocabulary.

LESSON 2
My body (pp. 30-31)

Objectives: Reinforce parts of the body. Develop fine motor skills. Revise vocabulary from the previous unit. Develop pre-reading and pre-writing skills.
Language focus: Move your (head). Stamp your feet.
Target vocabulary: head, arms, legs, feet, one, two, three, four, five, six, clown, teddy bear.
Vocabulary (revision): Classroom instructions. Colours.
Materials: Flashcards (head, arms, legs and feet). Flashcards of Unit 3. Class CD. Sheets of paper (extension activity).

19 Warm-up
Revise the chant of the previous lesson.

Begin the lesson by chanting and acting out the unit chant. Play the CD and encourage pupils to join in, clap the appropriate number of times when they hear the numbers, and do the actions.

Pupils' books open. Focus pupils' attention on the double spread. Play the CD again, asking them to follow the chant and point to the parts of the body as they hear them.

2 20 Listen, colour and trace. (p. 31)
Developing listening and writing skills.

Ask pupils to take out the following crayons: orange, red, blue and green. Show them the crayons one by one and elicit the colours: This is… (orange).
Point to the clown and say: This is a clown. Explain the activity: pupils colour the parts of the clown's body according to the audio. Remind them to mark the items with a dot of colour first and finish colouring when the listening is over. Play Track 20.

Audio script

Point to the head. Colour the head orange.
Point to the arms. Colour the arms red.
Point to the legs. Colour the legs blue.
Point to the feet. Colour the feet green.

Pupils trace the words. Go round the room to help pupils if necessary. Check the activity by holding up your book and pointing to each part of the clown. Say: Head and elicit: Orange. Do the same with the arms, legs and feet. Then do the opposite, saying the colours first and eliciting the parts of the body then.

Round-up

Activity Book (p. 23)

Trace, draw and say.
Developing observation and pre-writing skills.

Focus pupils' attention on the page. Point to the first teddy bear and say: This is a teddy bear. Ask: What's missing? Elicit: The head. Pupils then trace the word in pencil and draw the head. Do the same with the other teddies.
Go round the room to help pupils if necessary. When they have finished, hold up the finished page so they can check their work.

Reinforcement activity: Play 'Rocky says' to revise this lesson vocabulary (Resource File, TPR game 2, p. 77).

Extension activity: Play 'Count the claps' using the numbers 1-6 (Resource File, TPR game 4, p. 77).

LESSON 3

Let's sing and do! (p. 32)

Objectives: Present the parts of the face. Develop listening comprehension skills. Develop reading and writing skills. Sing the song and act it out.
Language focus: Point to the boy. I've got blue eyes. My dad's got blue eyes. I've got a small nose. My dad's got a small nose. Do I look like my (mum)?
Target vocabulary: eyes, nose, mouth, big, small.
Vocabulary (revision): Dad, Mum, brother, sister.
Materials: Flashcards (head, arms, legs, feet, eyes, nose and mouth). Class CD. One sheet of paper for each pupil (extension activity).

Warm-up
Present the words 'big' and 'small.'

Draw a large circle in the air and say: Big! Pupils do the same and repeat the word. Then draw a small circle and say: Small. Pupils draw a small circle and say: Small!
Point to large and small objects in the class and ask: Is it big or small? Elicit the answer each time, first chorally and then individually.

Pre-listening activity
Present 'eyes', 'nose' and 'mouth'.

Pupils' books closed. Draw a blank face on the board and ask: What's missing? In L1, elicit eyes, nose and mouth. Draw these parts of the face, saying the words in English. Pupils repeat chorally and individually.
Point to your own face and say: I've got two eyes, a nose and a mouth. Pupils do the same, pointing to their own eyes, nose and mouth.

1 21 **Let's sing and do! (p. 32)**
Sing and act out the unit song.

Pupils' books open. Focus pupils' attention on page 32. Pupils point to the characters as you name them. Say: Point to dad! Point to mum! Point to the boy! Present the song, using the CD and the book. Pupils listen and look at the pictures as you point to the pictures in your book. Say: Listen to the song!

Audio script

I've got blue eyes,
My dad's got blue eyes,

I've got a big mouth,
My mum's got a big mouth!

I've got a small nose,
My dad's got a small nose!

Do I look like my mum?
Do I look like my dad?

Play the song again, doing one of the following activities each time: **1** Pupils follow the song in their books, pointing to the characters in turn. Say: Listen and point. **2** Pupils point to their own eyes, nose and mouth when they hear the words. Say: Listen and do! **3** Divide the class into three groups, A, B and C. Hand out the flashcard of the eyes to group A, the nose to group B and the mouth to group C. Group A sings the first two lines while holding up the eye flashcard. Groups B and C then sing their lines while holding up their respective flashcards. Everyone joins in the chorus.
Finally, read the words at the bottom of the page, asking pupils to repeat them. Then say the words at random and ask pupils to point to the words as they hear them.

Round-up

Activity Book (p. 24)

Join the twins and say.
Developing observation skills and pronouncing the new words.

Focus pupils' attention on the page. In L1, tell pupils that each children in the first column has a twin in the second column. The task is to find and join each pair. Since twins usually look alike, they should look at their features carefully in order to match them correctly.

Point to the first face and say: Brother – he's got a big mouth! Trace the line down to his twin and say: Sister – she's got a big mouth!
Go round the room to help them if necessary. When pupils have finished, show them the completed page so they can check their work.

Reinforcement activity: Play 'Statues' using the following words: head, arms, legs, feet, eyes, nose, mouth. (Resource File, TPR game 7, p. 78)

Extension activity: Hand out one sheet of paper per pupil. Show the class how to fold them three times to make six squares. Tell them to number the squares 1-6. Dictate the following words dictation:
One. Draw a big nose. Two. Draw a small mouth. Three. Draw two small eyes. Four. Draw a big head. Five Draw two small feet. Six. Draw a big, big rabbit! When they have finished, pupils 'read' their drawings in pairs. Pupil A says: Four! Pupil B says: A big head!

LESSON 4
Draw and say. (p. 33)

Objectives: Sing the song and act it out. Reinforce the vocabulary of the unit. Develop observation and fine motor skills.
Language focus: He's got (big) eyes.
Target vocabulary: hands.
Vocabulary (revision): head, arms, legs, feet, eyes, nose, mouth, hands.
Materials: Flashcards (head, arms, legs, feet, eyes, nose and mouth). Class CD. A long piece of wrapping paper and magic markers (round-up activity).

Warm-up
Revise the unit song.

Begin the lesson by singing and acting out the unit song (p. 32). Play the CD.
Encourage pupils to point to their own eyes, nose and mouth when they hear the words.

4 My body

Preparing for the 'Draw and say' activity
Revise vocabulary.

Show pupils the lesson flashcards and elicit the words. Then play 'Correct Rocky' with the class. (Resource File, Flashcards game 3, p. 78)

Draw and say. (p. 33)
Developing observation and fine motor skills.

Focus pupils' attention on the page and ask: What's this? (A circus.) Say: Point to the clown. Point to his head / arms / legs / feet.
Point to the face of the first clown and ask: What's missing? Elicit: The eyes. Pupils then draw the eyes. Do the same with the faces of the two remaining clowns. Go round the room to help pupils if necessary. When they have finished, hold up the completed page so they can check their work.

Round-up
Revise the parts of the body and introduce the word 'hands.'

Hold up your hands and say: Hands! Look at my hands! Pupils hold up their hands and repeat the word. Give them additional instructions: Touch your hands. Clap your hands.
Stick the piece of wrapping paper across the board. Write the heading 'Our hands' across the top. Place your hand on the paper and outline it with the magic marker. Once finished, print your name under the drawing.
Call pupils up to the board, give them a magic marker and ask them to draw their hands and print their names underneath when they have finished.
Finally, count off the hands in groups of six with the class.

Reinforcement activity: Play 'Count the claps' with the numbers 1-6 (Resource File, Class game 4, p. 77).

Extension activity: Play 'Follow the leader' using the following instructions: Touch your (head). Clap your hands. Stamp your feet. (Resource File, Class game 10, p. 79)

LESSON 5
Let's listen! (p. 34)

Objectives: Associate spoken words with pictures. Develop observation skills. Revise vocabulary. Develop basic hygiene habits.
Language focus: Look, this is the head! Look at the legs! Here's my lunch. Thanks, mum! Stop! Wash your hands before lunch!
Vocabulary (revision): head, arms, hands, legs, feet, eyes, nose, mouth, chicken, apple, orange, banana, milk, table, chair, door, window, mum.
Materials: Flashcards of units 1-4. Class CD.

Warm-up
Revising vocabulary.

Show the pupils the flashcards of units 1-4 at random and check they remember the words. Then play 'Odd one out' (Resource File, Flashcards game 8, p. 79).

Pre-listening activity
Present the word 'wash'.

Pupils' books closed. Mime washing your hands and say: Washing … I'm washing my hand. Invite pupils to do the same and repeat the sentence. Then point to different pupils and say: (Elena), wash your hands, please. Elena does the action. Do this with several pupils.
In L1, ask pupils when they should wash their hands, and why it is important.

22 Let's listen! (p. 34)
Developing listening skills and vocabulary in context.

Focus pupils' attention on the scene. In L1, ask them to describe what is happening in the frames: Rocky is modelling a dog out of plasticine. His mother calls him for lunch but his hands are dirty.
Tell pupils to point to the following items: chicken, apple, orange, banana, milk, table, chair, door, window and mum.
Present the comic using the CD and your book. Say: Listen and look at the pictures!

Audio script

1 ROCKY   Look, this is the head!

2 ROCKY   And now, look at the legs!

3 ROCKY   Oh, here's my lunch. Thanks, mum!

4 ROCKY'S MUM Stop! Look at your hands!

5 ROCKY   Wash your hands before lunch!

Make sure that pupils understand the dialogues. Then play the comic again, doing one of the following activities each time: **1** Pupils follow the comic in their books pointing to each frame in turn. Say: Listen and point. **2** Pupils mime modelling the dog's head and legs in the first two frames; they show their dirty hands in frame 3 and wash them in frame 5. Say: Listen and do! **3** Play the CD again with pauses for them to repeat, chorally or individually. Check their pronunciation and intonation.

Round-up

Pupils act out the comic.

Divide the class into two groups and assign the roles of Rocky and his mum.
Play the CD again, with pauses after each line so that each group can repeat it and mime the actions. Then invite them to swap roles and repeat the activity.

Reinforcement activity: Read out different lines from the comic and elicit the character's name each time.

Extension activity: Ask pupils to draw other basic actions to keep clean and tidy, for example brushing their teeth, washing their hair, taking a shower, etc. Collect the drawings and make a display. When you take down the display, help pupils store their drawings in their Language Portfolio.

LESSON 6
Let's play Bingo! (p. 35)

Objectives: Revise and consolidate the vocabulary of this unit. Develop spoken interaction. Develop fine motor skills. Develop pre-reading, observation and memory skills.
Vocabulary (revision): head, arms, legs, hands, feet, eyes, nose, mouth.
Materials: Unit flashcards. Stickers. Nine tokens (or scraps of paper) for each pupil to play Bingo. Formative assessment sheet p. 99. Sheets of paper (extension activity).

Warm-up
Revise the unit vocabulary.

Show the unit flashcards one by one and elicit the words. Choose six flashcards and stick them on the left-hand side of the board. On the right-hand side, write the numbers from 1 to 6.
Say: Eyes – number four and draw a line joining the flashcard and the number. Pupils repeat chorally or individually.
Call different pupils to the board and say, for example: Hands – number three. The pupil matches the picture with the number. Encourage him/her to say the words. Repeat the activity several times, switching the flashcards around.

Preparing for the Bingo! (p. 35 and stickers)
Pupils complete the Bingo grid with stickers and revise vocabulary.

Focus pupils' attention on the page. Ask: What's this? (A robot.) Tell them that they are going to play Bingo once they have completed the grid with the appropriate stickers.
Pupils go to the stickers page and look for the hands sticker. When they find it, they remove it and stick it in one of the white circle on page 35. Stress that they can choose the circle where they want to stick it. Do the same with the stickers of the feet and arms.

Let's play Bingo! (p. 35)
Checking comprehension of the unit vocabulary.

Pupils identify the different parts of the robot. Tell them to focus on the completed robot as they must match the details of each square with the whole. (Answers: head, hands, eyes, nose, mouth, feet, legs, arms.) In L1, remind them of how to play Bingo! Hand out nine tokens to each pupil. Say the words at random slowly, repeating them twice. When the game is over, play again, asking a pupil to help you out.

Round-up
Developing spoken interaction.

Pupils play in pairs. One says the words and the other covers them. Then they swap roles. Go round the room to help them, if necessary, and/or assess speaking skills using the Formative assessment sheet p. 99

Reinforcement activity: Play 'Vanishing pictures' with the unit flashcards (Resource File, Flashcards game 11, p. 79).

Extension activity: Hand out one sheet of paper per pupil. Show the class how to fold it to make six squares (They have to fold it three times). Pupils make up their own Bingo grid using parts of the body and food items. Play with the class, holding up the appropriate flashcard as you call out the word.

LESSON 7
Stick, trace and join.
Activity Book (p. 25)

Objectives: Develop fine motor skills. Revise the unit vocabulary. Develop spoken expression.
Language focus: Point to the eyes. Point to the nose. Point to the mouth. Point to the hands.
Vocabulary (revision): head, arms, hands, legs, feet, eyes, nose, mouth. Colours.
Materials: Unit flashcards. Photocopies of Cut-out (p. 102). A completed page 25.

21 Warm-up
Revise the unit vocabulary and the song.

Begin the lesson by singing and acting out the unit song (p. 32). Play the CD and encourage everyone to join in.

Stick, trace and join.
Developing speaking and writing skills.

Focus pupils' attention on the page. In L1, explain that the children are watching a performance in a theatre: Who's on the stage? Elicit replies: A pirate? … A robot? … A clown? Let the pupils try a few times and then confirm that it is a clown.
Explain that they are going to complete the page by sticking the clown on the stage. Show them your finished page.
Hand out the photocopies of the cut-out page. Ask them to colour in the clown using colours that they know in English and then cut it out. Then, pupils go back to page 25 and complete the page.
Finally, pupils trace the words and join them to the corresponding parts of the clown's face and body. When they have finished, help pupils invent some lines for the clown to say, for example: Oh, I'm a funny clown. Look at my legs! I can dance, one, two, three!

Round-up
Display the finished pages.

Prepare a display of Activity Book pages for everyone to see their classmates' work.

[19] Reinforcement activity: Pupils repeat and act out the chant from lesson 1.

Extension activity: Play 'Red Rover' using the unit flashcards (Resource File, Flashcard game 9, p. 79).

LESSON 8
My world! (p. 36)

> **Objectives:** Associate spoken words with pictures. Develop listening comprehension skills. Revise vocabulary. Transfer the new language into an authentic context.
> **Language focus:** Hello, I'm Cathy. I look like my granny. I've got brown eyes, a small nose and a small mouth.
> **Vocabulary (revision):** Unit vocabulary. Colours.
> **Materials:** Unit flashcards. Number flashcards 1-6. Class CD.

Warm-up
Revise the vocabulary up to this unit.

Hand out the unit and number flashcards to different pupils and elicit the words. Say: Four – legs. Pupils holding the flashcards stand and show them to the class. To make the activity more fun, vary the rhythm of the instructions. If you speak slowly, pupils show the flashcards slowly, and viceversa.

[23] Listen and point. (p. 36).
Develop listening comprehension.

Focus pupils' attention on the page. Point to the girl and say: Look, this is Cathy. Point to the grandmother and say: This is her granny. Ask pupils to point to the appropriate persons as you name them. Say: Point to (granny).
Point to one person and say: Touch her nose! Touch her hand! Touch her head! etc. Ask pupils to do the same with a partner using other parts of the body.

Finally invite pupils to listen to Cathy speaking about her family. Play the CD.

Audio script

Hello, I'm Cathy. I look like my granny.
I've got brown eyes, a small nose and a small mouth.

Make sure pupils understand the expression look like. Play the CD again, doing one of the following activities each time: **1** Pupils listen and follow in their books, pointing to the parts of the face as they hear the words. Say: Listen and point. **2** Play the CD again with pauses for them to repeat, chorally or individually. Check their pronunciation and intonation.

Round-up

Activity Book (p. 26)

Draw, colour and say.
Developing observation skills and revising the colours.

Ask pupils to take out their pencils and crayons. Explain that they are going to complete the second half of each drawing by focusing on the empty squares on the right-hand side and observing the mirror image on the left in order to draw in the missing parts correctly. When they have finished, they colour in the drawings.
Go round the room to help pupils, if necessary. Ask individual pupils to identify the colours or the parts of the body they are drawing.

Reinforcement activity: In pairs, pupils give each other instructions, for example: Touch your legs! Touch your nose!

Extension activity: Help pupils create a display with photos of people who look alike. These can be cut out of magazines and mounted on poster paper. Write 'They look alike' as the poster title. Then ask different pupils to point to two faces on the poster and identify the members of the family that look alike or are the same colour. Help them say for example: He's got big eyes and she's got big eyes. She's got blue eyes and he's got blue eyes. Etc…

My body

LESSON 9
My turn! (p. 36)

> **Objectives:** Revise and consolidate the vocabulary and structures of Unit 4. Revise the unit song. Develop listening skills. Develop pre-reading and pre-writing skills. Do assessment and self-assessment activities.
> **Language (revision):** Structures of the unit.
> **Vocabulary (revision):** Unit vocabulary. Numbers 1-6.
> **Materials:** Five tokens or scraps of paper per child. Class CD. Unit flashcards.

(21) Warm-up
Revise the unit song and vocabulary.

Begin the lesson by singing and acting out the unit song (p. 32). Encourage pupils to join in and point to their own eyes, nose and mouth when they hear the words.

My turn! (p. 37)
Pupils give personal information using the language learnt.

Focus pupils' attention on the page. Point to the words at the bottom and read them. Pupils point to the words as they hear them.
Stick the unit flashcards on the board one by one. Elicit each word, then write it under the corresponding flashcard. Then play 'Words and pictures' (Resource File, Flashcard game 13, p. 80). Leave the flashcards on the board for the next activity.
Focus pupils' attention on the frame on page 37 and ask them to draw their self-portrait. When they have finished, they label their picture.
Go round the room to help them, if necessary. Ask individual pupils to identify the persons.

Round-up

Activity Book (p. 27)

Listen and find.
Developing listening skills and revising the unit vocabulary and numbers.

Focus pupils' attention on the page and explain the activity. Pupils have to put a token or a scrap of paper on one face in each row according to your instructions.
Hand out five tokens to each pupil. Point to the first row and say: This is a mouth. Repeat twice.
Do the same with the remaining rows, choosing one item each time.
Ask different pupils to identify the items they have covered to check comprehension.

End-of-unit sticker
Focus pupils' attention on the empty circle on the right-hand corner of the frame on page 37. Tell pupils that Rocky is happy because they have finished Unit 4 and ask them to peel off Rocky's sticker in the middle of the book and complete the page.

Reinforcement activity: Repeat the activity using different words (Activity Book, p. 27).

Extension activity: Pupils work in pairs. One pupil says the words and the other covers them. Then they swap roles.

Picture dictionary
Turn to page 43 and tell pupils they are going to revise the unit vocabulary orally and in writing. Point to the pictures in the sequence they are presented and ask pupils to identify them. Then vary the activity by pointing the activity at random. Finally, pupils trace over the words.

Testing and Assessment

Unit test
Photocopy Test 4 pages 93 and 94 and give a copy to each pupil. Pupils complete the test individually. Once you have corrected all the tests, return them to the pupils and help them check their performance by writing the answers on the board.
Record pupils' results on the End of unit assessment sheet (Resource File, p. 100). Make sure they file their tests in their Language Portfolio.

If you need to consolidate or develop this unit further, please turn to the Resource File (p. 77).

Unit 5 Animals

LESSON 1

Animals (pp. 38-39)

> **Objectives:** Recognise and name some animals. Develop fine motor skills. Reinforce the words big and small. To reinforce knowledge of the environment.
> **Language focus:** This is a (big bird). It says (tweet tweet).
> **Target vocabulary:** dog, cat, mouse, bird, pet.
> **Vocabulary (revision):** big, small. Colours.
> **Materials:** The following unit flashcards: dog, cat, mouse and bird. Class CD.

Warm-up

Revise 'big' and 'small.'

Read and explain the title of the unit.
Draw a big circle on the board and say: Big. Draw a small circle on the board and say: Small. Then trace a large circle in the air and repeat: Big. Do the same with the small circle. Repeat this several times and invite the pupils to join in. Pupils repeat chorally or individually.

Pre-listening activities (pp. 38-39)

Pupils familiarise with animal words and complete a scene with a sticker.

Pupils' books closed. Stick the flashcards of the dog, cat, mouse and bird on the board one by one. Say: I'm a dog. Woof! Woof! Encourage pupils to repeat chorally or individually. Do the same with the rest of the animals: I'm a bird. Tweet! Tweet! I'm a cat. Miaow! Miaow! I'm a mouse. Squeak! Squeak! Remove the flashcards from the board and stick them on different walls. Pupils imitate the animal sounds and point to the flashcard you indicate. Say: I'm a (bird)! Elicit: Tweet! Tweet! Repeat several times, increasing the speed and varying the order of the instructions.

Pupils' books open. Focus pupils' attention on the scene. Point to the characters and say: Look! Here are our friends … Elicit: Rocky, Freddy and Suzy. In L1 explain that they are in a pet shop. Explain the word pet. Pupils observe the scene and try to predict which animals are missing. Confirm that it is the birds. Show pupils the sticker of the birds and ask them to peel it off and stick it on page 38.

1 24 Let's chant. (pp. 38-39)

Pronouncing the new vocabulary.

Pupils' books open. Focus pupils' attention on the complete scene and describe the situation: The man is describing the animals in his shop.
Point to the animals and elicit the words bird, dog, cat, mouse. Then elicit the sizes: Big dog, small dog. Do the same with the rest of the animals. Pupils repeat chorally and individually as they point at the animals. Present the chant with the CD and the book.
Encourage pupils to listen and look at you while you point at the animals in your book. Say: Listen and look!

Audio script

This is a BIG bird.
It says TWEET! TWEET!
This is a small bird.
It says tweet! tweet!

This is a BIG dog.
It says WOOF! WOOF!
This is a small dog.
It says woof! woof!

This is a BIG cat.
It says MIAOW! MIAOW!
This is a small cat.
It says miaow, miaow!

This is a BIG mouse.
It says SQUEAK! SQUEAK!
This is a small mouse.
It says squeak! squeak!

Play the chant again, doing one of the following activities each time: **1** Pupils mime big or small when they hear the words. Say: Listen and mime. **2** Pupils point to the animals in their books. Say: Listen and point. **3** Pause after each verse and encourage pupils to repeat. Say: Listen and repeat!

Round-up

Activity Book (p. 28)

Join and circle.
Recognising animals, their size and their homes.

Pupils go to page 28 of the Activity Book. In L1, explain that they are going to identify the size of the animals and their 'homes'.
Give an example using the one provided. Point to the dog and the circled word and say: This is a big dog. Then follow the line and show them the big doghouse. Tell the pupils to do the same with the other animals. While the pupils are working, go round the room and ask individual pupils to identify the animals, their size and point at their homes.

Reinforcement activity: Play 'Chinese Whispers' using the lesson flashcards (Resource File, Flashcards game 1, p. 78).

Extension activity: Divide the class into four groups and assign one animal to each group: bird, dog, mouse and cat. Each group sings and mimes the animal while the others clap in time.

LESSON 2
Animals (pp. 38-39)

Objectives: Recognise and name some animals through a chant. Recognise animal silhouettes. Reinforce 'big' and 'small.'
Language focus: This is a (big bird). It says (tweet tweet).
Vocabulary (revision): Dog, cat, mouse, bird, big, small. Colours. Vocabulary of units 1-4 (extension activity).
Materials: Flashcards: dog, cat, mouse and bird. Class CD. Flashcards of units 1-4 (extension activity).

24 Warm-up
Revise the chant.

Begin the lesson by chanting and acting out the unit chant (pp. 38-39). Play the CD and encourage everyone to join in.

Pupils' books open. Focus pupils' attention on the double spread. Play the CD again, asking them to follow the chant and point to the animals as they are named.

2 25 Listen, join and say. (p. 39)
Developing listening skills and reinforcing animals.

Read the words and ask pupils to repeat them. Explain the activity: pupils join the animals with their silhouettes. Then they listen and repeat the sentences. Play Track 25.

Audio script

This is a dog … and that is a dog.
This is a cat … and that is a cat.
This is a mouse … and that is a mouse.
This is a bird … and that is a bird.

Go round the room in order to help pupils if necessary. Check their work by naming each animal and point at the corresponding silhouette. Say: This is a dog and elicit: That's a dog. Do the same with the other animals.

Round-up

Activity Book (p. 29)

Find, colour and trace.
Developing observation and pre-writing skills.

Pupils go to page 29 of the Activity Book. In L1, explain that they are going to find and colour four animals. First ask them to identify the animals at the top. Say: This is a… Elicit (cat).
Then say: Find the (cat). Tell them to choose the colour of the cat according to the model. Say: Colour the (cat). Go round the room to help pupils, if necessary. Ask individual pupils to identify the animals.

Reinforcement activity: Play 'Pass it on' with the unit flashcards (Resource File, TPR game 3, p. 77).

Extension activity: Play 'Odd one out ' using the flashcards of the units 1-5 (Resource File, Flashcards game 8, p. 79).

LESSON 3
Let's sing and do! (p. 40)

> **Objectives:** Present more animals. Develop listening comprehension skills. Develop pre-reading and pre-writing skills. Sing the song and act it out.
> **Language focus:** Who are you? I'm (Rocky the raccoon).
> **Target vocabulary:** raccoon, squirrel, fox, rabbit, seven, eight.
> **Vocabulary (revision):** dog, cat, bird, mouse.
> **Materials:** The unit flashcards. Class CD. One sheet of paper per pupil (reinforcement activity).

Warm-up
A TPR activity to revise the new vocabulary.

Stick the flashcards of the dog, cat, mouse and bird on the board one by one and elicit the words. Pupils repeat chorally and individually.
Point to the dog, mime and say: I'm a dog. Woof!

Woof! Repeat several times and encourage pupils to imitate you. Do the same with the other animals. Pupils repeat chorally and individually.

Pre-listening activity
A TPR activity to prepare for the song.

Pupils' books closed. Stick the flashcards of the fox, squirrel, raccoon, and rabbit on the board one by one and pronounce the words. Pupils repeat them chorally and individually.
Hand out the unit flashcards to different pupils. Point to one pupil and say: Who are you? Encourage the pupil to answer: I'm a (fox)! Ask the same question to all the pupils holding a flashcard.
Once finished with this lot, pupils pass their flashcards to someone else. Repeat the procedure.

1 26 Let's sing and do! (p. 40)
Pupils sing a song and act it out.

Pupils' books open. Focus pupils' attention on page 40. Pupils point to the animals as you name them. Say: Point to the (fox)! Confirm that Freddy is a fox. Do the same with the other animals: Suzy Squirrel, Rocky Raccoon, Robby Rabbit.
Present the song, using the CD and the book. Pupils listen and look at the pictures as you point in your book. Say: Listen to the song and look!

Audio script

CHORUS	Who are you? Who are you?
FREDDY	F-F Freddy Fox, Freddy Fox, I'm Freddy the fox!
CHORUS	Who are you? Who are you?
SUZY	S-S Suzy Squirrel, Suzy Squirrel, I'm Suzy the squirrel!

Animals

CHORUS   Who are you?
             Who are you?

ROCKY   R-R
             Rocky Raccoon,
             Rocky Raccoon,
             I'm Rocky the raccoon!

CHORUS   Who are you?
             Who are you?

ROBBY   R-R
             Robby Rabbit,
             Robby Rabbit,
             I'm Robby the rabbit!

Play the song again, doing one of the following activities each time: **1** Pupils follow the song in their books, pointing to each animal in turn. Say: Listen and point. **2** Stick the flashcards of the fox, squirrel, raccoon and rabbit on different walls. Pupils do the actions with you while pointing to the flashcards. Say: Listen and do! **3** Pupils dance in place as they sing along. Say: Sing and do! **4** Divide the class into four groups and assign the roles of Freddy, Rocky, Suzy and Robby. Each group sings and acts out the corresponding lines while the others clap in time. Finally, read the words at the bottom of the page and ask pupils to repeat them. Then repeat the words at random and ask pupils to point to the words as they hear them.

Round-up

Activity Book (p. 30)

Count and say.
Practising counting to eight.

Begin by counting on your fingers in time from 1 to 8. Say: One, two, three… eight. Encourage pupils to do the same. Then, invite them to count books, pencils, chairs and tables from 1 to 8 only.
Pupils go to page 30 of the Activity Book. In L1, explain that they are going to count the animals in the scene. Point to the first box at the bottom of the page and ask: What's this? Elicit: A raccoon. Do the same with the other animals.

Pupils count the animals and write the number in the appropriate box.
Go round the room to help pupils with the activity. Check the activity by naming each animal and eliciting the number. Say: Raccoons and elicit: Five? Three? Four? Wait for pupils to call out and confirm a number and say: Yes, four! Do the same with the other animals.

Answers: 4 raccoons; 8 rabbits; 3 foxes; 6 squirrels.

Repeat the procedure, saying the number first and then eliciting the corresponding animal.

Reinforcement activity: Hand out a sheet of paper to each pupil. Ask them to choose and draw one of the character of the song. Play the song again (Track 26). Pupils do the actions with you, raising their drawings when they hear their character named. Say: Listen and do!

Extension activity: Play 'Pass it on' with the whole class using the unit flashcards (Resource File, TPR game 3, p. 77).

LESSON 4
Find and colour. (p. 41)

Objectives: Sing the song and act it out. Reinforce the vocabulary of the unit. Solve a puzzle.
Language focus: Who are you? I'm (Freddy the fox).
Vocabulary (revision): dog, cat, mouse, bird, fox, squirrel, raccoon, rabbit. Parts of the body and food.
Materials: The unit flashcards. Class CD. Crayons. Flashcards of units 3 and 4 (extension activity).

Warm-up
Revise the unit song on page 40.

Stick the flashcards of Freddy, Suzy, Rocky and Robby on different walls. Begin the lesson by the unit song. Play the CD. Encourage everyone to join in and point to the flashcards as they hear the animals.

Play 'Statues' with the whole class using the parts of the body (Resource File, TPR game 7, p. 78).

Preparing for the 'Find and colour' activity
Pupils revise the unit vocabulary.

Draw the following animal silhouettes on the board: a mouse, a rabbit, a fox, a squirrel and a raccoon. Pupils identify them. Then point to each one and say the corresponding word. Encourage pupils to repeat chorally and individually. Finally point to the silhouettes at random and elicit the words.

Find and colour.
Developing observation skills.

Focus pupils' attention on the page. In L1, explain that they are going to find and colour some animals in the drawing. First, they identify the animals at the top.
Point and say: Who's this? Elicit: Freddy the fox, Suzy the squirrel, Rocky the raccoon, Robby the rabbit and Mr Mouse.
Pupils observe the drawing to find Freddy the fox and when they have found it, they colour it in. Pupils do the same with the other characters.
While pupils are working, go round the class and ask individual pupils to identify the animals.
Check the activity with the whole class by pointing in your book and saying: This is (Freddy the fox).

Round-up

A game to check comprehension of the unit vocabulary.

Play 'Let's dance' using the unit flashcards (Resource File, TPR game 8, p. 78).

Reinforcement activity: Play 'Correct Rocky!' with the unit flashcards (Resource File, Flashcards game 3, p. 78).

Extension activity: Play 'Odd one out' with the whole class using the flashcards of units 3, 4 and 5 (Resource File, Flashcards game 8, p. 79).

LESSON 5
Let's listen! (p. 42)

> **Objectives:** Associate spoken words with pictures. Develop observation skills. Revise vocabulary. Developing attitudes of respect towards animals.
> **Language focus:** Is it a (mouse)? It's a rabbit.
> **Target vocabulary:** baby, bird.
> **Vocabulary (revision):** cat, mouse, dog, bird, fox, squirrel, raccoon, rabbit, mouse.
> **Materials:** Unit flashcards. Class CD. A picture of baby birds cut out from a magazine. Sheets of paper (extension activity).

Warm-up
Revise the unit vocabulary.

Play 'What's missing?' using the unit flashcards (Resource File, Flashcards game 4, p. 78).

Pre-listening activity
Present the word 'baby bird' and the comic.

Pupils' books closed. Stick the magazine cut-out of the baby birds on the board and present the words baby and birds. Pupils repeat chorally and individually. Play 'Twist around' using the complete set of the unit flashcards (Resource File, TPR game 5, page 77).

27 Let's listen! (p. 42)
Developing listening comprehension skills.

Focus pupils' attention on the scene. In L1, ask them to describe what is happening in the frames: Rocky, Suzy and Freddy are looking at animal tracks in the woods. Tell pupils to point to the birds and the rabbits. Say: Point to the (birds)!
Present the comic using the CD and your book. Say: Listen and look at the pictures!

Audio script

1 FREDDY Look! Is it a mouse?
   SUZY   Is it a rabbit?
   FREDDY No, no!

2 FREDDY   Look, it's a bird. A big bird! And baby birds!

3 ROCKY   Look! Is it a mouse?
  SUZY   No, no!

4 SUZY   Look, it's a rabbit! A rabbit and baby rabbits! Shhh …

5 SUZY   Don't disturb baby animals!

Make sure that pupils understand the dialogues. Then play the comic again, doing one of the following activities each time: **1** Pupils listen and follow the comic in their books, pointing to each frame in turn. Say: Listen and point. **2** Stick the flashcards of the bird and the rabbit on different walls. Pupils point to the flashcards when they hear the words. Say: Listen and do! **3** Play the CD again with pauses for them to repeat, chorally or individually. Check their pronunciation and intonation.

Round-up

Pupils act out the comic.

Divide the class into three groups and assign the roles of Freddy, Suzy and Rocky. Give each group the flashcard of a character.
Play the CD again, with pauses after each line so the groups can repeat it and mime the actions. If you have time, swap roles and repeat the activity.

Reinforcement activity: Read out different lines from the comic and ask pupils who is speaking. If necessary, help them by eliciting the character's name.

Extension activity: Ask pupils to draw some baby animals they like. On the board, write: Don't disturb baby animals! Pupils copy the sentence at the top of their pictures. Collect the drawings and make a display. When you take down the display, help pupils store their drawings in their Language Portfolio.

LESSON 6

Let's play Bingo! (p. 43)

Objectives: Revise and consolidate the vocabulary of this unit. Develop spoken interaction. Develop fine motor skills. Develop pre-reading, observation and memory skills.
Language focus: What's this? (A dog).
Vocabulary (revision): Cat, dog, bird, mouse, fox, squirrel, raccoon, rabbit.
Materials: Unit flashcards. Stickers. Nine tokens (or scraps of paper) per pupil to play Bingo. Formative assessment sheet (Resource File, p. 99).

Warm-up
Revise the unit vocabulary.

Show the unit flashcards one by one and elicit the words, then play 'What's missing?' (Resource File, Flascards game 4, p. 78)

Preparing for the Bingo! (p. 43 and stickers)
Pupils revise the animals and complete the grid with the stickers.

Focus pupils' attention on the page. Tell the pupils that they are going to play Bingo after they have completed the grid with the appropriate stickers. Pupils predict which animals are missing: the bird, the squirrel and the rabbit.
Pupils go to the stickers page and look for the bird. When they have found it, they peel it off and stick it in one of the white circle on page 43. Do the same with the stickers of the squirrel and the rabbit.

Let's play Bingo! (p. 43)
Developing listening skills and recognising the unit vocabulary.

Focus pupils' attention on the page. Ask them to identify some of the animals in the squares. Point and ask: What's this? Elicit: A (dog). Pupils repeat chorally or individually.

In L1, remind them of how to play Bingo! Hand out nine tokens to each pupil. Say the words at random slowly twice, for example: A raccoon. When the game is over, play again, asking a pupil to help you.

Round-up

Developing spoken interaction.

Pupils play in pairs. One says the words and the other covers them. Then they swap roles. Go round the room to help them, if necessary, and/or assess their speaking skills using the Formative assessment sheet.

Reinforcement activity: Play the 'Twist around' with the unit flashcards (Resource File, TPR game 5, p. 77).

Extension activity: Give pupils a few moments to memorise page 43. Stress that they have to focus on the position of the animals. Then draw a bingo grid on the board and number the squares 1-9 going from left to right. Pupils' books closed, point to a square and ask: What's in square (3)? Elicit: A bird. Pupils check the answers by looking at the page.

LESSON 7
Stick, colour and say.
Activity Book (p. 31)

> **Objectives:** Develop fine motor skills. Revise the unit vocabulary. Develop spoken interaction.
> **Language focus :** Who are you? I'm (Freddy the fox).
> **Vocabulary (revision):** rabbit, bird, mouse, raccoon, dog, squirrel, fox, cat.
> **Materials:** Unit flashcards. Photocopies of Cut-out pp. 103 and 104. Your finished page 31 from the Activity Book.

26 Warm-up
Revise the unit song on page 40.

Begin the lesson by singing and acting out the unit song. Play the CD and encourage everyone to join in.

Stick, draw and say.
Developing spoken interaction.

Focus pupils' attention on the page. Say: This is a computer. Point to the animals at the bottom and elicit the name of the first animal. Ask pupils to trace the word under the picture. Do the same with the other animals. Then read the words and ask pupils to repeat them chorally and individually.
Explain that they are going to complete the page by gluing in the frame of the computer screen and moving a strip of animals back and forth across it. Show them your finished page.
Hand out the photocopies. Pupils cut out the frame of the computer screen and the animal strip. They identify and colour the animals. Then, show them how to stick the frame on the computer and how to move the animal strip back and forth.

Guessing Game
Developing spoken interaction.

Pupils play in pairs. They take it in turns to 'call up' an animal on their screen, cover it and ask their partner: What is it? The partner guesses the animal, then they swap roles. Go round the room to help pupils, if necessary, and/or assess speaking skills using the Formative assessment sheet.

Round-up

A class display with the finished pages.

Prepare a display of Activity Book pages for pupils to see their classmates' work.

24 Reinforcement activity: Pupils repeat the chant and point to animals on page 38.

Extension activity: Play 'Chinese Whispers' with the whole class using the unit flashcards (Resource File, game 1, p. 78).

5 Animals

LESSON 8
My world! (p. 44)

Objectives: Associate spoken words with pictures. Develop listening comprehension skills. Revise vocabulary. Transfer the new language into an authentic context.
Language focus: I love animals. I've got a (rabbit).
Vocabulary (revision): Animals, food and parts of the body.
Materials: Unit flashcards. Flashcards of units 3 and 4. Class CD. Pictures of pets cut out from magazines (extension activity).

Warm-up
Revise the vocabulary taught so far.

Play 'Odd one out' with the whole class using the flashcards of units 3, 4 and 5 (Resource File, Flashcards game 8, p. 78). To engage the pupils more, ask them to select the flashcards.

28 Listen and point. (p. 44)
Developing listening comprehension skills.

Focus pupils' attention on the page. Point to the boy in picture 3 and say: Look, he's got two dogs, a big dog and a small dog. Then say: Point to the (big) dog. Point to the girl in picture 1 and say: Look, she's got a… rabbit. Then point to the girl in picture 2 and say: Look, she's got a… dog.
Finally, invite pupils to listen to the children speaking about their pets. Play the CD.

Audio script

1 I love animals. I've got a rabbit.

2 I love animals. I've got a small dog.

3 I love animals. I've got a small dog and a big dog.

Play the CD again, doing one of the following activities each time: **1** Pupils listen and follow in their books,

pointing to the animals as they hear the words. Say: Listen and point. **2** Play the CD again with pauses for them to repeat, chorally or individually. Check their pronunciation and intonation.

Round-up

Activity Book (p. 32)

Draw, colour and circle.
Developing observation and reading skills.

Ask pupils to take out their pencils and crayons. Explain that they are going to complete the second half of each drawing by focusing on the empty squares on the right-hand side and observing the mirror image on the left-hand side in order to draw in the missing lines correctly. When they have finished, they colour the drawings.
Once completed the drawing, they circle the word that corresponds to the animal above.
Go round the room to help pupils with the activity. Ask individual pupils to identify the animals and the colours they are using.

Reinforcement activity: Pupils go to page 44 of the Pupils' Book and work in pairs. They give each other instructions, for example: Touch the rabbit! Touch the big dog!

Extension activity: Help pupils create a display with photos of pets. These can be cut out of magazines and mounted on poster paper. Write 'Animals' or 'Pets' as the poster title. Then ask different pupils to point to an animal on the poster and identify it. Help them say: This is a (rabbit).

LESSON 9
My turn! (p. 45)

Objectives: Revise and consolidate the vocabulary and structures of Unit 5. Revise the unit song. Develop listening skills. Develop pre-reading and pre-writing skills. Do assessment and self-assessment activities.
Language (revision): Structures of the unit.
Vocabulary (revision): Unit vocabulary.
Materials: Five tokens or scraps of paper per child. Class CD. Unit flashcards.

26 Warm-up
Revising the unit song and vocabulary.

Stick the flashcards of Freddy, Suzy, Rocky and the Robby on different walls. Begin the lesson by singing the unit song (p. 40). Play the CD. Encourage everyone to join in and point to the flashcards as they hear the animals.

My turn! (p. 45)
Pupils give personal information using the language they have learnt.

Focus pupils' attention on the page. Point to the words at the bottom and read them. Pupils point to the words as they hear them.
Stick the unit flashcards on the board one by one. Elicit each word, then write it under the corresponding flashcard. Then play 'Words and pictures' (Resource File, game 13, p. 80). Leave the flashcards on the board for the next activity.
Focus pupils' attention on the frame on page 45 and ask them to draw and colour their favourite animal. When they have finished, they write the name of the animal underneath.
Go round the room to help them with the activity. Ask individual pupils to identify the animals.

Round-up

Activity Book (p. 33)

Listen and find.
Developing listening skills and identifying animals.

Focus pupils' attention on the page and explain the activity. Pupils have to put a token or a scrap of paper on one animal in each row according to your instructions. Hand out five tokens to each pupil. Point to the first row and say: This is a rabbit. Repeat twice.
Do the same with the remaining rows, choosing one animal each time.
Check their comprehension by asking different pupils to identify the animals they have covered.

End-of-unit sticker
Focus pupils' attention on the empty circle on the right-hand corner of the frame on page 45. Tell pupils that Rocky is happy because they have finished Unit 5 and ask them to peel off Rocky's sticker in the middle of the book and complete the page.

Reinforcement activity: Repeat the activity on page 33 (AB) using different words.

Extension activity: Now pupils work in pairs. One pupil says the words and the other covers them. Then they swap roles.

Picture dictionary
Turn to page 44 and tell pupils they are going to revise the unit vocabulary orally and in writing. Point to the pictures in order and ask pupils to identify them. Then point to the pictures at random and do the same. Finally, pupils trace over the words.

Testing and Assessment

Unit test
Photocopy Test 5, pages 95 and 96, and give a copy to each pupil. Pupils complete the test individually. Once you have corrected all the tests, return them to the pupils and help them check their performance by writing the answers on the board.
Record pupils' results on the End of unit assessment sheet (Resouce File, p. 100). Make sure they file their tests in their Language Portfolio.

If you need to consolidate or develop the unit further, please turn to the Resource File (p. 77).

My holidays

My holidays (pp. 46-47)

Objectives: Recognise and name some summer clothes and accessories. Understand and use the prepositions on and under. Develop fine motor skills. Develop pre-reading and pre-writing skills.
Language focus: Where's my rucksack? Where are my shorts? Under the bed. On your head.
Target vocabulary: holidays, rucksack, shorts, sandals, sunhat, silly.
Vocabulary (revision): Classroom objects and furniture.
Materials: Photo of a summer scene for example at the beach. Flashcards (rucksack, sandals, shorts and sunhat). Class CD.

Warm-up

Introduce the new topic.

In L1, tell pupils that in this unit is about summer holidays. Present and explain the word 'holidays.' Ask them when they have holidays (Christmas, Easter, the summer or winter break, etc.), where they go and what they do.

Pre-listening activities. (pp. 46-47)

Present the new vocabulary. Pupils complete a scene with a sticker.

Pupils' books closed. Pin up the photo of the holiday scene you have brought and elicit pupils' comments in L1. Ask: Do you like holidays? Then point any rucksacks, sandals, shorts and sunhats in the scene and present the words.
Stick the flashcards of the rucksack, sandals, shorts and sunhat on the board. Point to each one in turn and say the words. Pupils repeat chorally and individually.

Pupils' books open. Focus pupils' attention on the scene. Point to the characters and elicit their names.

Ask: Where are they? (In the bedroom.) Ask pupils to point to: bed, table, chair, window, book and crayons. Pupils observe the whole scene and try to predict what is missing. It is something on Rocky's head. Confirm that it is the sunhat.
Tell pupils to peel off the sticker and stick it on page 46 to complete the scene.

1 29 **Let's chant. (pp. 46-47)**
Developing listening and speaking skills.

Pupils' books open. Focus pupils' attention on the scene and describe the situation: Rocky is preparing for the holidays. He is tidying up his room and getting his summer things together.
Present the chant with the CD and the book. Encourage pupils to listen and look at you while you point to Rocky, Freddy and Suzy in succession. Say: Listen and look!

Audio script

ROCKY   My rucksack, my rucksack,
        Where's my rucksack?

FREDDY Under the bed!

ROCKY   My shorts, my shorts,
        Where are my shorts?

FREDDY Under the bed!

ROCKY   My sandals, my sandals,
        Where are my sandals?

FREDDY Under the bed!

ROCKY   My sunhat, my sunhat,
        Where's my sunhat?

SUZY   On your head, silly!

Play the chant again, doing one of the following activities each time: **1** Pupils listen and point to the rucksack, shorts, sandals and sunhat in their books. Say: Listen and point. **2** Pupils mime under and on when they hear the words. Say: Listen and do. **3** Pause after each verse and encourage pupils to repeat. Say: Listen and repeat!

Round-up

Activity Book (p. 35)

Find, colour and trace.
Develop observation and fine motor skills.

Pupils go to page 34 of the Activity Book. Point to the words and pictures at the top of the page and read them aloud. Pupils point and repeat, then trace each word.
Pupils find and colour the objects in the drawing. Go round the room to help pupils with the activity. Ask individual pupils to identify the objects and their colours. When they have finished, show them the completed page so they can check their work.

Reinforcement activity: Say the chant while pointing to the pictures in the Pupil's Book. Repeat a second time inviting pupils to complete your sentences, for example:
Teacher: My rucksack, my rucksack. Where's my rucksack?
Pupils: Under the bed!

Extension activity: Pupils play in pairs with a crayon, a rubber and a pencil. They take it in turns to put it on or under a larger object (a book, their table or their chair) and ask: Where's my (crayon)? Their partner answers the question and asks another one.

LESSON 2
My holidays (pp. 46-47)

Objectives: Reinforce the vocabulary of the previous lesson. Count to 10. Develop fine motor skills. Revise vocabulary from the previous units. Develop pre-reading and pre-writing skills.
Language focus: Where's my rucksack? Where are my shorts? Under the bed. On your head.
Target vocabulary: rucksack, shorts, sandals, sunhat, ball, train, seven, eight, nine, ten.
Vocabulary (revision): Numbers 1-6. Classroom objects.
Materials: Flashcards (rucksack, shorts, sandals, sunhat, ball). Flashcards of numbers 1-10. Class CD.

29 Warm-up
Revise the chant.

Begin the lesson by chanting and acting out the unit chant (pp. 46-47). Play the CD and encourage pupils to join in and mime the prepositions.
Show the flashcards (rucksack, shorts, sandals, sunhat and ball) one by one and elicit the words. Present the word ball. Stick the flashcards on the board and play 'Vanishing pictures' (Resource File, Flashcards game 11, p. 79).

Pupils' books open. Focus pupils' attention on the double spread. Say: Point to the sunhat. Point to the ball. Point to the window. Vary the rhythm of the instructions.

2 30 Listen and colour. (p. 47)
Developing listening comprehension skills. Revising colours.

Ask pupils to prepare the following crayons: yellow, green and blue. Show them the crayons one by one and elicit the colours: This is… (green).
Explain the activity: pupils listen to the CD and colour in the items according to what they hear. Remind them to mark the items with a dot of colour first and finish colouring when the listening is over. Play Track 30.

6 My holidays

Audio script

It's a yellow rucksack.
The shorts are blue.
The sandals are green.
It's a green sunhat.

Go round the room to help pupils with the activity. Check their work by holding up your book and pointing to each item. Say: The rucksack is … and elicit: Yellow. Do the same with shorts, sandals and sunhat. Then reverse the procedure, saying the colours first and eliciting the corresponding items.

3 31 Count. (pp. 46-47)

Developing listening and reading skills.
Practising the pronunciation of a few numbers.

Point to the train on page 46 and say: This is a train. Pupils repeat chorally. Point to the numbers on the cars and count aloud to 10. Encourage pupils to count with you.
Then point to the numbers 7, 8, 9 and 10 on page 47. Pupils count aloud as they read the words. Finally, play the CD so they can check their pronunciation.

Audio script

Seven   Nine
Eight   Ten

Round-up

Activity Book (p. 34)

Count, trace and join.
Pupils practise counting to 10 and develop pre-writing skills.

Begin by counting on your fingers slowly. Say: One, two, three, … ten. Encourage pupils to do the same. Then invite them to count up to 10 tables and chairs in the room.
Pupils go to page 34 of the Activity Book. In L1, explain that they are going to count some objects.
Point to the items in the circles and explain that they have to count and join them to the corresponding

number on the right. When they have done this, they trace the number words. Go round the room to help pupils with the activity.

Reinforcement activity: Hand out the number flashcards to ten pupils. Count to 10 together with the class and tell them to hold up the flashcard corresponding to the number they hear.
Then call them out to the front of the room and ask them to reorganise themselves in the sequence 1-10 while the rest of the pupils count aloud. Repeat the activity with different pupils.

Extension activity: Pupils stand up in pairs: one is the 'writer' and the partner is the 'page.' The 'Pages' close their eyes and turn their backs to the 'writers.' Write a number between 1 and 10 (in letters) on the board or hold up the appropriate number of fingers. 'Writers' trace this number on the 'pages' who must identify it and say it aloud.

LESSON 3

Let's sing and do! (p. 48)

Objectives: Present the word happy. Develop listening comprehension skills. Develop observation skills. Sing the unit song and act it out.
Language focus: We're going away on holiday. Are you happy? Yes, we're happy.
Target vocabulary: sunglasses, camera, electronic game, happy, sad.
Vocabulary (revision): rucksack, sunhat, shorts, sunhat, ball, bird, mouse, rabbit.
Materials: Unit flashcards. Flashcards of units 1 and 3. Class CD. One sheet of paper per pupil (extension activity).

Warm-up

Presenting new objects and talking about holidays.

Take out the flashcards of the camera, sunglasses and electronic game and present the words. Pupils repeat chorally and individually.
Show the pupils a few flashcards of units 1 and 3 to

check if they remember the previous vocabulary. Then say: I'm going on holiday. What do I need? Call pupils up to your table and ask them to select a flashcard each time. Repeat: I'm going on holiday. Then add: I need a (sunhat). I need (sunglasses). I need a (book), etc. until they have selected all the items they think are necessary.

Pre-listening activity
Present the words 'happy' and 'sad.'

Make a happy face and say: I'm happy! Pupils do the same and repeat. Then make a sad face and say: I'm sad! Pupils make a sad face and repeat: I'm sad! Invite pupils to mime a happy or sad expression according to your instructions. Elicit the adjective each time, first chorally and then individually.

32 **Let's sing and do! (p. 48)**
Pupils sing the unit song and act it out.

Pupils' books open. Focus pupils' attention on page 48. Say: Point to Rocky. Point to the mouse. Point to the birds. Then ask: Are they happy? Why? Confirm that they are happy because they are going on holiday. Present the song, using the CD and the book. Pupils listen and look at the pictures as you point at them in your book. Say: Listen to the song and look!

Audio script

Hurray, hurray,
We're going away,
We're going away,
On holiday!

Rocky, are you happy?
Suzy, are you happy?
Freddy, are you happy?

Yes, we're happy!
We're happy and …

Hurray, hurray,
We're going away,
We're going away,
On holiday!

Play the song again, doing one of the following activities each time: **1** Pupils listen and look at scene in their books, pointing to the characters in turn. Say: Listen and point. **2** Pupils mime happy when they hear the word. Say: Listen and do! **3** Divide the class into two groups. Group A sings the verses and group B sings the chorus.

Round-up

Activity Book (p. 36)

Look, draw the mouth and say.
Developing observation skills and practising the new vocabulary.

Focus pupils' attention on the page. Point to frame 1 and ask: What's missing? Elicit that it is the girl's mouth. In L1, tell pupils to observe the other scenes and decide if the children are happy or sad.
Give an example of what they have to do by pointing to the girl's face in picture 1 and asking: Is she happy? Is she sad? Trace a happy mouth and say: She's happy! Pupils complete the children's face of the remaining pictures.
Go round the room to help them, if necessary. When pupils have finished, check their work by pointing to each frame in turn and elicit happy or sad.

Reinforcement activity: Play 'Red Rover' using the unit flashcards (Resource File, Flashcards game 9, p. 79).

Extension activity: Hand out the sheets of paper to the pupils and ask them to draw themselves in a holiday scene. Write the heading My holidays on the board so they can copy it on their drawing. Collect the drawings and make a display. When you take down the display, help pupils store their drawings in their Language Portfolio.

My holidays

vocabulary of units 1-5 (Resource File, Production game 3, p. 78).

LESSON 4

Draw the mouth and say: happy or sad? (p. 49)

Objectives: Sing the song and act it out. Reinforce the vocabulary learnt so far. Develop observation and fine motor skills.
Language focus: He's happy. He's sad.
Vocabulary (revision): rucksack, sunhat, shorts, sandals, sunglasses, ball, camera, electronic game, happy, sad. Vocabulary of units 1-5.
Materials: Class CD. Sheets of paper (round-up and extension activity).

32 Warm-up
Revise the unit song.

Begin the lesson by singing and acting out the unit song (p. 48). Play the CD.
Encourage pupils to mime happy when they hear the word.

Draw the mouth and say: happy or sad? (p. 49)
Developing observation and fine motor skills.

Focus pupils' attention on page 49. In L1, explain that all the frames have been taken from previous comics. Point to frame 1 and ask: What's missing? Elicit that it is Rocky's mouth. Help pupils locate the comic and the frame in their books. Point to the frame and ask: Is Rocky happy or sad? (Happy.) Go back to page 49 and tell them to draw a happy mouth on Rocky's face.
Pupils do the same with the remaining three frames. Go round the room in order to help them if necessary. When pupils have finished, point to each frame in turn and elicit: Rocky is happy or Rocky is sad. Finally, ask them to tell you where the remaining frames are in the book.

Round-up

Do a 'Picture dictation' using the unit vocabulary (Resource File, Production Games 4, p. 78).

Reinforcement activity: Play 'Add a word' with the

Extension activity: Hand out the sheets of paper to the pupils and ask them to draw a situation that makes them either happy or sad. Write the headings I'm happy and I'm sad on the board. When they finish, they copy the appropriate sentence on their drawing. Collect the drawings and make a display. When you take down the display, help pupils store their drawings in their Language Portfolio.

LESSON 5

Let's listen! (p. 50)

Objectives: Associate spoken words with pictures. Develop observation skills. Revise vocabulary. Acquire and reinforce the concept of sharing things with our neighbours.
Language focus: Look at my camera! Hey, let me see. No, don't touch it! I'm sorry! Let's play together! OK, you're right. Share with your friends. It's more fun!
Vocabulary (revision): camera, sunglasses, electronic game, ball, shorts, sandals, sunhat. Vocabulary of units 1-5.
Materials: Unit flashcards. Flashcards of units 1-5. Class CD.

Warm-up
Revising vocabulary.

Show the pupils a few flashcards of units 1-6 to check if they remember the vocabulary taught in previous lessons. Then play 'Odd one out' (Resource File, Flashcards games 8, p. 79).

Pre-listening activity
Talk about sharing things with the others.

Pupils' books closed. Stick the unit flashcards on the board and elicit the words. In L1, ask pupils if they share their things with their friends. Call individual pupils up to the board and ask them to point to two items that they would share with their friends.

Encourage them to say: My (ball) and my (electronic game).
In L1, ask pupils why it is more fun to share with their friends.

🎧33 Let's listen! (p. 50)
Developing listening/comprehension skills.

Focus pupils' attention on the comic. In L1, ask them to describe what is happening in the frames: Rocky is showing Suzy and Freddy his new camera. Freddy wants to play with it but Rocky doesn't let him.
Tell pupils to point to the sunhat and the shorts.
Present the comic using the CD and your book. Say: Listen and look at the pictures!

Audio script

1 ROCKY   Look at my camera! One, two, three, cheese!

2 FREDDY   Hey, let me see.
   ROCKY   No, don't touch it!

3 FREDDY   Oh no!
   ROCKY   No!

4 FREDDY, ROCKY, SUZY   Oh!

5 SUZY   Now, let's play together!
   FREDDY   OK, you're right. I'm sorry Rocky!

6 SUZY   Say cheese!
   FREDDY, ROCKY   Cheese!

Make sure that pupils understand the dialogues. Then play the comic again, doing one of the following activities each time: **1** Pupils listen and follow the comic in their books, pointing to each frame in turn. Say: Listen and point. **2** Pupils mime showing the camera and taking a picture in frame 1, dropping it in frame 3 and looking at it on the ground in frame 4. Say: Listen and do! **3** Play the CD again with pauses for them to repeat, chorally or individually. Check their pronunciation and intonation.

Round-up

Pupils act out the comic.

Divide the class into three groups and assign the roles of Rocky, Freddy and Suzy.
Play the CD again, with pauses after each line so the groups can repeat it and mime the actions. Then swap the roles and repeat the activity.

Reinforcement activity: Read out different lines from the comic and ask pupils who says them. You can help them by eliciting the character's name each time.

Extension activity: Ask pupils to draw a scene in which they share something with a friend. Collect the drawings and make a display. When you take down the display, help pupils store their drawings in their Language Portfolio.

LESSON 6
Let's play Bingo! (p. 51)

Objectives: Revise and consolidate the vocabulary of the unit. Develop spoken interaction. Develop fine motor skills. Develop pre-reading, observation and memory skills.
Vocabulary (revision): rucksack, sunhat, shorts, sandals, ball, camera, sunglasses, electronic game.
Materials: Unit flashcards. Flashcards of the book and the pencil (unit 1). Stickers. Eight tokens (or scraps of paper) per pupil to play Bingo. Formative assessment sheet (Resource File, p. 99). Sheets of paper and flashcards of unit 5 (extension activity).

Warm-up
Revise vocabulary.

Show the unit flashcards and the flashcards of the book and the pencil one by one, eliciting the words. Stick them on the left-hand side of the board. On the right-hand side, write the numbers from 1 to 10.
Say: Rucksack – number four and draw a line joining the flashcard and the number. Pupils repeat chorally or individually.
Call different pupils to the board and say, for example: Sunglasses – number nine. The pupil joins the two.

Encourage him/her to say the words. Repeat the activity several times, switching the flashcards around.

Let's play Bingo! (p. 51)
Developing listening skills and checking comprehension of the unit vocabulary.

Pupils identify the different items and numbers in the grid. In L1, remind them of how to play Bingo! Hand out eight tokens to each pupil. Say the words at random slowly, repeating them twice. When the game is over, play again, asking a pupil to help you.

Round-up

Developing spoken interaction.

Pupils play in pairs. One says the words and the other covers them. Then they swap roles. Go round the room to help them if necessary and/or assess speaking skills using the Formative assessment sheet.

Reinforcement activity: Play 'Let's dance' with the unit flashcards (Resource File, TPR game 8, p. 78).

Extension activity: Hand out the sheets of paper, one per pupil. Show the class how to fold them three times to make six squares. Pupils make up their own Bingo game using the unit vocabulary and animals. Play with the class, holding up the appropriate flashcard as you call out the word.

LESSON 7

Trace, stick and say.

Activity Book (p. 37)

Objectives: Develop fine motor skills. Revise the unit vocabulary. Develop spoken interaction. Developing pre-writing skills.
Language focus: Look! I've got a (ball) and a (camera).
Vocabulary (revision): Unit vocabulary. Colours.
Materials: Unit flashcards. Photocopies of Cut-out (p. 103). Your finished page 37 from the Activity Book.

32 Warm-up
Revise the unit vocabulary and song.

Begin the lesson by singing and acting out the unit song (p. 48). Pupils can pull a sad or happy face when they hear these words. Play the CD and encourage everyone to join in.

37 Trace, stick and say.
Developing pre-writing, fine motor skills and spoken interaction.

Focus pupils' attention on the page. In L1, explain that the boy and the girl are playing on the beach. Point to each one in turn and elicit what they are wearing (shorts). Explain that they are going to complete the page by tracing the words in the white circles and then sticking pictures over them. Show them your finished page. Hand out the photocopies of page 103. Pupils colour and cut out the ball, the sunhat, the electronic game and the camera. Tell them to use only one colour for each item. Then they go back to page 37 and complete the page.

Guessing game
Developing spoken interaction.

Pupils play the following memory game in pairs:
Pupil A: Has he got a (camera)?
Pupil B: Yes.
Pupil A: Is it (red)?
Pupil B: No.
etc.
Go round the class to check pronunciation and or assess speaking skills using the Formative assessment sheet.

Round-up
Display the finished pages.

Prepare a display of Activity Book pages for everyone to see their classmates' work.

Reinforcement activity: Write the unit vocabulary on the board, leaving out all the vowels. Pupils check the correct spelling in their Pupil's Book and complete the words in their notebooks.

Extension activity: Stick the unit flashcards on the board with the reverse side facing the pupils. Call pupils to the board one by one and say: Give me the (camera), please. They turn over one flashcard. If it is correct, they say: Here is the camera, and stick it back on the board with the picture showing. If it is incorrect, they stick it back where it was. Call another pupil out and continue the game until all the flashcards have been revealed.

LESSON 8
My world! (p. 52)

> **Objectives:** Associate spoken words with pictures. Develop listening comprehension skills. Revise vocabulary. Transfer the new language into an authentic context.
> **Language focus:** Hurray! It's holiday time! I'm on holiday with my mum and dad. I'm wearing a sunhat, shorts and sandals. I've got my camera.
> **Vocabulary (revision):** Unit vocabulary. Colours.
> **Materials:** Unit flashcards. Class CD.

Warm-up
Revise the vocabulary taught so far.

Hand out the unit and colour flashcards to different pupils and elicit the words. Say: Blue – sandals. Pupils holding the flashcards stand and show them to the class. To make the activity more fun, vary the rhythm of the instructions. If you speak slowly, pupils show the flashcards slowly, and vice versa.

34 Listen and point. (p. 52)
Developing listening comprehension skills.

Focus pupils' attention on the page. Point to the girl and say: Look, she's on holiday! Ask: What is she wearing? Elicit: A sunhat, shorts and sandals. Ask: Has she got a ball? (No.) Has she got an electronic game? (No.) What has she got? (A camera.)
Invite pupils to listen to the girl speaking about her family. Play the CD.

Audio script

Hurray! It's holiday time! I'm on holiday with my mum and dad. I'm wearing a sunhat, a T-shirt, shorts and sandals… and I've got my camera!

Play the CD again, doing one of the following activities each time: **1** Pupils listen and look at the picture in their books, pointing to the sunhat, the T-shirt, the shorts, the sandals and the camera when they hear the words. Say: Listen and point. **2** Play the CD again with pauses for them to repeat, chorally or individually. Check their pronunciation and intonation.

Round-up

Activity Book (p. 38)

Draw and write.
Developing fine motor and pre-writing skills.

Pupils take out their pencils and crayons. Ask them to identify the three items (a camera, an electronic game, sunglasses). Tell them to trace over the dotted lines to complete all three items. When they have finished, they colour the drawings.
Go round the room to help pupils with the activity. Ask individual pupils to identify the colours they use.

Reinforcement activity: Play 'Guess the flashcard' with the unit flashcards (Resource File, Flashcards game 12, p. 79).

Extension activity: Help pupils create a display with photos of holiday scenes. These can be cut out of magazines and mounted on poster paper. Write 'On holiday!' as the poster title. Then ask different pupils to point and name the items they can identify on the poster.

My holidays

LESSON 9
My turn! (p. 53)

> **Objectives:** Revise and consolidate the vocabulary and structures of Unit 6. Revise the unit song. Develop listening skills. Develop pre-reading and pre-writing skills. Do assessment and self-assessment activities.
> **Language (revision):** Structures of the unit.
> **Vocabulary (revision):** Unit vocabulary. Numbers 1-10.
> **Materials:** Tokens or scraps of paper, five per child. Class CD. Unit flashcards.

32 Warm-up
Revise the unit song and vocabulary.

Begin the lesson by singing and acting out the unit song (p. 48). Encourage everyone to join in.

My turn! (p. 53)
Pupils give personal information using the language they have learnt.

Focus pupils' attention on the page. Point to the words at the bottom and read them. Pupils point to the words as they hear them.
Stick the unit flashcards on the board one by one. Elicit each word, then write it under the corresponding flashcard. Then play 'Words and pictures' with the class (Resource File, Flashcards game 13, p. 80).
Leave the flashcards on the board for the next activity.
Focus attention on the rucksack. Ask pupils to draw three items they would take with them on holiday.
At the end, they label their drawings.
Go round the room in order to help pupils with the activity. Ask individual pupils to identify the objects.

Round-up

Activity Book (p. 39)

Developing listening comprehension skills and consolidating the unit vocabulary.

Focus pupils' attention on the page and explain the activity. Pupils have to put a token or a scrap of paper on one of the items in each row according to your instructions.
Hand out five tokens to each pupil. Point to the first row and say: This is a book. Repeat twice.
Do the same with the remaining rows, choosing one item each time.
Check their comprehension by asking different pupils to identify the items they have covered.

End-of-unit sticker
Focus pupils' attention on the empty circle on the right-hand corner of the rucksack on page 53. Tell pupils that Rocky is happy because they have finished Unit 6 and ask them to peel off Rocky's sticker in the middle of the book and complete the page.

Reinforcement activity: Repeat the activity on page 39 (AB) using different words.

Extension activity: Now pupils work in pairs. One pupil says the words and the other covers them. Then they swap roles.

Picture dictionary
Turn to pages 45 and 46 of the Activity Book and tell pupils they are going to revise the unit vocabulary orally and in writing. Point to the pictures in order and ask pupils to identify them. Then point to the pictures at random and do the same. Finally, pupils trace over the words.

Revision (p. 58)

Let's colour!
Revising some vocabulary of Merry Team 1. Developing reading comprehension and memory skills.

Turn to page 58 in the Pupil's Book and point to the stones. Encourage pupils to read the word in each one. Then point to the box at the bottom of the page and read out the name of the first topic: My room. Ask pupils to identify the colour associated with it (red). Explain pupils that they have to find all the stones containing a word that is related to My Room and outline them in red. Pupils do this individually or in pairs. When they have finished, they read out the words so they can check their work.

Do the same with the other topics.

Testing and Assessment

Unit test

Photocopy Test 6 on pages 97 and 98, and give one copy to each pupil. Pupils complete the test individually. Once you have corrected all the tests, return them to the pupils and help them check their performance by writing the answers on the board. Record pupils' results on the End of unit assessment sheet (Resource File, p. 100). Make sure they file their tests in their Language Portfolio.

If you need to consolidate or develop the unit further, please turn to the Resource File (page 77).

The GINGERBREAD MAN

Pages 54-55

Objectives: Listening to a story in English for pleasure. Develop observation skills. Consolidate the vocabulary of units 4-6. To talk about helping others.

Language focus: What a nice surprise! What's that, Granny? A gingerbread man for you and me! Oh, what a yummy snack! Two eyes for the gingerbread man! A nose and a mouth for the gingerbread man! Jump, gingerbread man! Jump and run! Let's go away! Thank you, little bird! Thank you! Gingerbread man, go!

Vocabulary (revision): Members of the family, animals, parts of the body, holiday things.

Materials: Flashcards of units 4-6. Class CD.

Warm-up

Revise and consolidate vocabulary.

Take out the flashcards of units 4-6 and shuffle them. Tell pupils you are going to check if they remember the vocabulary of previous units. Choose 12 flashcards at random and place them face down on your desk. Show the flashcards one by one and instruct pupils to raise their hands if they know the word. Call on one pupil to say it aloud. If it is correct, write a tick on the board. If it is incorrect, ask another pupil. The activity ends when the pupils have identified all 12 flashcards and you have 12 ticks on the board.

1 Look and find. (p. 54)

Developing observation skills and pre-listening activities.

Pupils' books open. Focus pupils' attention on the double page. Read the title and explain that they are going to hear about a brave little gingerbread man. Point to the rabbit, the fox and the mouse. Tell pupils these animals are somewhere in the frames. Pupils observe the frames carefully in order to find them (mouse: frame 3; rabbit: frame 5; fox: frame 7.)

2 35 Let's listen to the story! (pp. 54-55)

Developing listening comprehension skills and consolidating the language.

Focus pupils' attention on the story frames and ask them to describe what is going on: A granny has baked a gingerbread man for her grandchildren. The gingerbread man doesn't want to be eaten and runs away. A little bird helps him escape.

Ask: Where is granny? Where is grandad? Where is the cat? And the dog? In frame 2, has the gingerbread man got eyes? In frame 4, is he happy? Is he happy in frame 8? Play the CD. Pupils listen and follow the story in their books.

Audio script

1	GRANNY	Hello, Tessa, hello Timmy! What a nice surprise!
2	TESSA	What's that, Granny?
	GRANNY	A gingerbread man for you and me!
	TIMMY	Oh, what a yummy snack!
3	GRANNY	Two eyes for the gingerbread man! A nose and a mouth for the gingerbread man!
4	BIRD	Jump, gingerbread man! Jump and run!
5	GRANDPA	What a yummy snack!
	BIRD	Run, gingerbread man! Run!
6	CAT	Meow! Meow! What a yummy snack!
	BIRD	Run, gingerbread man! Run!
7	DOG	Woof! Woof! What a yummy snack!
	BIRD	Run, gingerbread man! Run!
8	BIRD	Jump, gingerbread man! Let's go away!
	GINGERBREAD MAN	Thank you, little bird! Thank you!

Song

BIRDS   Run, run, run,
            Gingerbread man, run!
            Jump, jump, jump,
            Gingerbread man, jump!

            Run and jump!
            Run and jump!
            Gingerbread man, GO!

Ask pupils to explain why everyone is chasing after the gingerbread man. Why does the bird carry him across the river? Do you also help friends in trouble? How? Play the CD, doing one of the following activities each time: **1** Pupils listen and point to the frames in their books. Say: Listen and follow the story in your books!

2 Pause after each frame, encouraging pupils to repeat the dialogue. Say: Listen and say!

Round-up

Developing listening skills and checking comprehension.

Retell the story frame by frame, changing the following words: in frame 2, say mum instead of granny.
In frame 3, say face instead of eyes, nose and mouth.
In frame 6, say woof woof instead of meow meow.
In frame 7, say eek eek instead of woof woof. In frame 8, say little raccoon instead of little bird.

Note: Turning the stories into one-act plays. Ideas in the Resource file, page 80.

Christmas

Page 56

Objectives: Talk about Christmas. Develop listening comprehension skills. Develop fine motor skills. Develop pre-writing skills. Sing a Christmas song and act it out.
Language focus: We wish you a Merry Christmas! And a Happy New Year!
Vocabulary: Christmas tree, present.
Vocabulary (revision): red, yellow, blue, green.
Materials: A large Christmas tree made out of green paper for the class. White cards. Class CD. Cut-out, pages 61-62 (Pupil's Book).

Warm-up
Introducing the word Christmas.

Clap your hands in time as you recite the following chant quite slowly:

Merry Christmas!
Merry Christmas!
Merry Christmas
to everybody!

Encourage pupils to repeat, clapping their hands or tapping on their desks with one finger. Repeat the chant, speeding up the rhythm.

Pre-listening activity
Present the vocabulary related to Christmas.

Pin up the big Christmas tree you have prepared and say: Christmas tree. Pupils repeat chorally. Present the word present by drawing a present on the big Christmas tree. Pupils look, listen and repeat after you chorally and individually.

1 🔊 **Let's sing and colour. (p. 56)**
Pupils sing 'We wish you a Merry Christmas.'

Focus pupils' attention on the illustrations. Point to characters and elicit their names. Describe the situation: They are decorating the Christmas tree. Present the song, using the CD and the book. Pupils listen and look at the pictures as you point in your book. Say: Look and listen to the song!
Make sure that pupils understand the meaning of the song.

Audio script

We wish you a Merry Christmas!
We wish you a Merry Christmas!
We wish you a Merry Christmas!
And a Happy New Year!

Play the song again, making pauses so that pupils can learn it. Say: Listen and sing! Then, divide the class into two groups, one group singing the song to the other group. Then they swap roles.

Round-up

Pupils colour in the presents to complete the illustration and revise colours.

Point to the presents at the bottom of the page and tell pupils that they are going to colour them. Ask them to take out the following crayons: red, blue, yellow and green. Show them the crayons one by one and elicit the colours: This is… (red).
Pupils follow your instructions. Say: Show me red … yellow … blue … green. Do this several times, varying the order and the rhythm.
Explain the activity: pupils colour the presents while they listen and sing 'We wish you a Merry Christmas'. Finally, tell pupils that they are going to decorate the class Christmas tree. Hand out the white cards. Tell pupils to draw one present and colour it.
Invite pupils to come to the board and stick their presents on the Christmas tree anywhere they choose. Help them say: This is my present. It is (red).

Activity Book (pp. 61-62)

Christmas cut-out
Developing fine motor and pre-writing skills.

Pupils take out their scissors. Ask them to identify the illustration (a decorated Christmas tree) and count the presents aloud. Tell them to cut out the page and trace over the Christmas wish. They can complete the card by decorating it as they please and signing it. Go round the room to help pupils with the activity. Ask individual pupils to identify the colours they use. They can either take these cards home or exchange them with their friends in class.

Easter

Page 57

Objectives: Talk about Easter. Develop listening comprehension skills. Develop fine motor skills. Develop pre-writing skills. Say a chant and act it out.
Language focus: Easter egg! Look at you!
Vocabulary: Easter egg.
Vocabulary (revision): red, yellow, blue, green.
Materials: Class CD. Cut-out pages 63-64 (Pupil's Book).

Warm-up
Introducing the word Easter.

Clap your hands in time as you recite the following chant quite slowly:

Happy Easter!	Happy Easter!
Happy Easter!	to everybody.

Encourage pupils to repeat, clapping their hands or tapping on their desks with one finger. Repeat the chant, speeding up the rhythm.

Pre-listening activity
Present the word 'Easter egg'.

Draw a large Easter egg on the board and say: Look! This is an Easter egg. Pupils repeat chorally. Colour the Easter egg using red, yellow, blue, green and orange. As you colour, say each colour you are using. Pupils look, listen and repeat after you chorally and individually.

1 🎵37 **Let's chant and colour. (p. 57)**
Practising pronunciation.

Focus pupils' attention on the illustration. Point to the characters and elicit their names. Describe the situation: They are painting the Easter eggs and Rocky is painting himself as well.
Present the chant, using the CD and the book. Pupils listen and look at the pictures as you point in your book. Say: Look and listen to the chant!

Audio script

Easter eggs,	Look at you!
Red and yellow,	Red and yellow,
Easter eggs!	Look at you!
Green and blue,	Green and blue.

Play the chant again, doing one of the following activities each time: **1** Pupils follow the chant in their books, pointing to the colours. Say: Listen and point. **2** Make pauses so pupils can chant. Say: Listen and chant! **3** Divide the class into two groups. One group chants the first stanza and the second group chants the chorus. Then they swap roles.

Round-up

Pupils colour in the Easter egg to complete the illustration and revise colours.

Point to the white Easter egg at the bottom of the page and tell pupils that they are going to colour it. Ask them to take out the following crayons: red, blue, yellow, orange and green. Show them the crayons one by one and elicit the colours: This is… (red). Pupils follow your instructions. Say: Show me red … yellow … orange … blue … green. Do this several times, varying the order and the rhythm.
Explain the activity: pupils colour the Easter egg while they listen and chant the Easter chant. Finally, invite pupils to come to the board and show their books. Help them say: This is my Easter egg. It is (yellow and blue).

Activity Book (p. 63-64)

Easter cut-out
Developing fine motor and pre-writing skills.

Pupils take out their scissors. Ask them to identify the items in the illustration (a rabbit with an Easter basket full of Easter eggs) and count the eggs aloud with them. Tell them to cut out the page and trace over 'Happy Easter' (page 64) and complete the card by decorating it and sign their name.
Go round the room to help pupils with the activity. Ask individual pupils to identify the colours they use.
They can either take these cards home or exchange them with their friends in class.

Resource File

INTRODUCTION

This Resource File provides a variety of extra games and activities for you to use in the classroom. Games form part of children's daily activities and experience. Through games children socialise, interact with the other children, relax and have fun. This enables them to lower their affective filters and use the language more naturally. To help you choose the most appropriate activity for your lesson, games and activities have been grouped as follows:

• TPR (Total Physical Response) games / games for recognition
These games are intended to expose pupils to the language. Pupils are simply expected to demonstrate comprehension of the language through movement.

• Games for production
These are simple, guided games that allow pupils to use the vocabulary they have learnt.

• Flashcards games
Flashcards inspire a wide variety of games.

• Turning the stories into one-act plays
In this section you will find ideas on how you can dramatise the stories in the Pupil's Book, to consolidate the language learnt in the previous lessons. Using drama techniques will also help pupils develop spoken interaction and self-confidence.

• Photocopiable instruments for assessment
Assessment is an integral part of the learning process and it is most successful when done through the systematic observation of pupils during the course.

• Activities with the cut-outs
These photocopiable pages provide the missing elements needed to complete the Stick, draw and say pages in the Activity Book.

TPR (TOTAL PHYSICAL RESPONSE) GAMES – GAMES FOR RECOGNITION

1 Touch red
The aim of this game is to recognise colours. In L1,

explain to pupils that when you say a colour, they have to touch something in the colour you pronounced. Say: Stand up, please! Touch red! and do the action. Do the same with the other colours they know. Repeat the game several times.

2 Rocky says
This game is an adaptation of 'Simon says.' The aim is to recognise and follow simple instructions. Say: Stand up. Touch your (legs). Touch (blue). Pupils have to do the actions only if the instruction is preceded by the words 'Rocky says…' Use this game to revise classroom instructions and vocabulary.
2a You can play the same game using the word please instead of Rocky says.

3 Pass it on
The aim of this game is to recognise objects when they are named. Pupils stand around in a circle or at their desks if the class is large. Hand out different objects to different pupils (for example, classroom objects). Pupils pass them on to their neighbour on the right or the left. Signal the beginning of the game by saying Ready, steady, go! or by playing music. Stop the game by saying Stop! or by stopping the music. Say: Show me the (crayon)! Show me the (book)! Pupils holding the objects hold and show them up to the class. Then the game starts again.

4 Count the claps
The aim of this game is to count and say the numbers. Tell pupils to close their eyes. Think of a number they have learnt and clap your hands the same number of times. Pupils count silently and raise their hands when they are ready to answer. Write it on the board for everyone to check.

5 Twist around
The aim of this game is to recognise objects. Ask pupils to place different objects around the classroom (for example classroom objects). Then tell them to stand and point to the objects as quickly as they can as you name them. Say: Point to the (book). Pupils twist around and point to the objects in front of them, behind or sideways. To make the game more fun, vary

the rhythm of the instructions. If you speak slowly, pupils move slowly, and vice versa.

6 In the bag
The aim of this game is to identify objects by touch them. Place several small objects in a bag (for example classroom objects, pieces of fruit, plastic animals). Go round the room and invite different pupils to give you the objects you specify. Say: Give me the (pencil), please. They put their hand in the bag and draw out the appropriate item. Encourage them to say: Here it is!

7 Statues
Pupils form a circle. Play some music and ask them to dance. Stop the music and say: Touch your face! Tell them that when the music stops they have to follow the instruction (touch their face) and stand still like statues till the music plays again. Play the music another time and say: Touch your head! Touch your mouth! etc. Do this several times.

8 Let's dance!
Tell pupils they are going to dance. Hand out the flashcards of a lexical set to different pupils and explain that they have to pass them on to other children when the music starts playing. Play the music and say: Let's dance! Pupils dance and pass the flashcards around. Stop the music and say: Show me the (biscuit). The pupil holding the biscuit flashcard holds it up for everyone to see. Do this several times, calling out different flashcards.

PRODUCTION GAMES

1 Up and down
The aim of this game is to recognise and say the numbers. Tell pupils they are going to guess numbers 1 to (10). Think of a number and write it on a piece of paper. Pupils take it in turns to guess the number you have written. To help them, say and mime: Up! if the number is too low or Down! if it is too high, until they guess.

2 Odd one out
The aim of this game is to recognise words belonging to the same lexical set. Pick three words from the same set and one word from a different one. Say the words slowly, for example: Eyes, bed, nose, mouth. Pupils raise their hands when they have identified the odd one out and say it aloud.

3 Add a word
A variation on the previous game. Say three words from any lexical set and encourage different pupils to add a fourth word belonging to that same set.

4 Picture dictation
Hand out one sheet of paper to each pupil. Help pupils fold them three times in order to make six squares. Ask them to number the squares while saying: One, two, three, four, five, six. Tell pupils that they are going to draw six objects, one in each square. Say: Draw a (window). Draw a (crayon). etc. Pupils draw the item in any square they wish. When they have finished, divide the class into pairs. Pupils ask each other questions without looking at their partners' sheet, for example: Is number 4 a (window)? or What is number (4)?

FLASHCARDS GAMES

1 Chinese Whispers
Pupils form a circle. Give a flashcard from a lexical set to the first pupil without the others seeing it. He or she whispers the corresponding word to the next pupil and so on. The last pupil in the circle calls out the word and the first pupil reveals the flashcard to check. Start with a different pupil each time. This game helps you monitor pronunciation.

2 Echo Game
Stick the unit flashcards on the board and elicit the words. Tell pupils that they are going to be your echo and will have to repeat the words you say in the same way. Say the words slowly, fast, sadly, angrily, happily, loudly and in a whisper. This game is particularly useful to practise pronunciation and intonation.

3 Correct Rocky!
Show pupils the flashcards of a lexical set and elicit the words. Put them down on your table, pick up the Rocky puppet and say: Rocky, give me the (book). Rocky picks the wrong flashcard. Say: No, no, Rocky! Ask a pupil to help Rocky pick the correct flashcard. Play again with a different flashcard and different pupils.

4 What's missing?
The aim of this game is to discover the missing flashcard. Show pupils one set of flashcards and elicit the words as you stick the flashcards on the board.

Give them a minute to look at them, then tell them to close their eyes. Remove one flashcard and ask pupils: What's missing? Encourage them to tell you which flashcard is missing. Then shuffle the flashcards and play again. To make the game more challenging, remove two flashcards.

5 Who/What is it?
Place the unit flashcards on your desk. Ask a pupil to stick one of the flashcards on the board. Turn your head in order not to see it, then ask pupils: Is it the (apple)? Is it the (banana)? etc. Pupils reply yes or no until you guess the correct word. Ask another pupil to come up to the board and pick a different flashcard, and play again. Depending on the level of the class, you may try having a pupil guessing the flashcards on the board.

6 Pass the flashcards
Hand out the flashcards of one or two lexical sets and play some lively music. While it is playing, pupils pass their flashcard along. When it stops, each pupil holding a flashcard names it. If they can't remember the word they pay a forfeit, for example singing a song, miming an animal or doing an action. Demonstrate this yourself first.

7 Sequences
The aim of this game is to have pupils remember sequences of flashcards. Take out the flashcards of a lexical set and show them one by one eliciting the words. Repeat the words in the same order several times, then ask pupils to repeat them. Show them the flashcards in order to confirm their answers. Collect the flashcards, shuffle them and play again.

8 Odd one out
The aim of this game is to recognise words in the same lexical set. Choose several flashcards that belong to the same set and one that doesn't. Say all the words slowly and clearly while flashing the corresponding card. Pupils listen and raise their hands to say which word is the odd one out.

9 Red Rover
Select one set of flashcards, for example food. Divide the class into as many groups as there are flashcards. Hand out a flashcard to the leader of each group. Check that pupils know which group they belong to by

saying: (Apple!) Pupils in the apple group raise their hands. The groups of pupils stand together on one side of the room with the leader holding the flashcards. Stand on the opposite side and say the following rhyme: Red Rover, Red Rover, let the (apples) come over. The apple group runs or walks over to your side. Call out another food item and keep playing until all the groups are on your side. Then name new leaders, switch sides and start the game again.

10 Follow the leader
Stick one set of flashcards, for example food, around the room. Ask pupils to stand up and form a queue behind you. When they are ready, ask them to follow you, counting and doing the actions according to your instructions. Say: Let's play 'Follow the leader'! Walk around the room with them. Take three steps forward and say: One, two, three, clap your hands. Four, five, six, point to the (chocolate). Take another three steps forward and give another order, for example: One, two, three, touch your (feet). Four, five, six, point to the (milk). Vary the rhythm of the steps in order to make the activity more fun.

11 Vanishing pictures
The aim of this game is to remember words. Stick up to six flashcards on the board in two rows. Point to them in the same order and say the words three times. Encourage pupils to repeat. Remove one flashcard and repeat the words again, including the missing flashcard. Remove another card and do the same. Continue until all the flashcards have vanished. At the end of the game, pupils should be able to repeat all the words in the correct order as you point to the empty spaces on the board.

12 Guess the flashcard
The aim of this game is to identify pictures. Use one set of flashcards or flashcards from different sets if you want to play a really challenging game. Cover one card with a piece of paper and move the paper slowly in any direction to reveal details of the picture. As soon as pupils recognise the item, they raise their hands and then say the word aloud.

12a Upside down flashcard
Hold the flashcards upside down or sideways while playing.

13 Words and pictures

Show pupils several flashcards one by one, and elicit the words as you stick them on the board. Write the word under each flashcard. Then, invite pupils to associate words with pictures. Remove all the flashcards and leave the words on the board. Shuffle the flashcards and give one to a pupil. Ask him or her to stick it next to the corresponding word. Do the same with all the flashcards.

TURNING THE STORIES INTO ONE-ACT PLAYS

General indications

First, assign roles to pupils. It is recommended to rehearse in class a few lines at a time. This can be done by listening, pausing and repeating. You can also ask pupils to listen to the story on their Pupil's CD at home and rehearse their lines on their own. When working with the group, always check rhythm and intonation and encourage pupils to speak slowly and articulate the words properly.

In the following lessons, pupils act out their lines in groups. If there are more children than parts, any 'extra' pupils can act as a chorus for the song and as an 'echo' to the important lines. The role of the chorus should be enhanced by handing out musical and/or percussion instruments to the pupils, to be played at appropriate moments.

STORY 1

Cast: Narrator, Lucky, Jimmy, Jenny, Monty, Mum, Chorus.

Suggested props
• Cut-outs of the biscuit, of the banana and of the chocolate bar (Pupil's Book p. 59), or realia: a packet of biscuits, a banana and a chocolate bar.
• A football.
• Two chairs representing a park bench.
• A table set for lunch, and a chair for Lucky.
• Flashcards of chicken and milk.

Suggested scenery:
A fingerpainted backdrop of sky and greenery.
A fingerpainted backdrop of a door and window.

PLAY

Narrator: Let's listen to the story.
/dramatic tone/ I'm hungry!

Lucky enters first, kicking a football.
Jimmy follows, munching on a biscuit. Lucky goes up to him.

Lucky: Hey, Jimmy, I'm hungry! I'm really hungry!
Chorus: Hey, Jimmy, I'm hungry! I'm really hungry!

Jimmy looks at him and hands him a biscuit (or offers him the packet of biscuits).
Jimmy: Here's a biscuit for you!

Lucky takes it.
Lucky: Oh thanks, Jimmy!

Jenny enters, carrying bags with her shopping. Lucky goes up to her.

Lucky: Hey, Jenny, I'm hungry! I'm really hungry!
Chorus: Hey, Jenny, I'm hungry! I'm really hungry!

Jenny looks at him and hands him a banana.
Jenny: Here's a banana for you!

Lucky takes it.
Lucky: Oh thanks, Jenny!

Monty enters, munching on a chocolate bar. Lucky goes up to him.

Lucky: Hey, Monty, I'm hungry! I'm really hungry!
Chorus: Hey, Monty, I'm hungry! I'm really hungry!

Monty looks at him and hands him some chocolate.

Monty: Here's some chocolate for you!
Lucky takes it.
Lucky: Oh thanks, Monty!
/props change quickly – we are now in Lucky's kitchen/

Mum enters and calls to Lucky.
Mum: Lunch is ready, Lucky.
Lucky sits at the table and looks over his lunch.
Lucky: My favourite lunch! Thanks, Mum!

Lucky hasn't moved. Suddenly, he pushes his plate away.
Lucky: Oooh, I'm not hungry. Sorry, Mum, I'm not hungry!
Chorus /sad/: Sorry, Mum, I'm not hungry!

The entire cast and chorus sing the first verse of the song, Lucky's mum shaking her finger at him throughout.

Chorus   If you are hungry,
             Don't nibble,
             Don't nibble,
             Wait for lunch,
             Please!

Mum then comes forward and sings the second verse with the backing of the chorus. She points to the table while she sings.

Mum   Lunch is on the table,
             Chicken, milk and fruit,
             Lunch is on the table,
             Lunch is waiting for you!

Then the actors and chorus take a bow and wave goodbye to the audience.

STORY 2

Cast: Narrator, Gingerbread Man, Tessa, Timmy, Granny, Grandad, Bird, Cat, Dog, Chorus.

Suggested props
• Oven mitts and apron for granny.
• A straw hat for grandad.
• A bowl and spoon.
• A baking sheet.
• Cut-out of the gingerbread man (Pupil's Book, p. 59).
• A bowl of coloured chocolate 'Smarties' (or coloured buttons).

• A chair and a table for granny's kitchen.
• Flashcards of the dog, cat and bird (alternatively makeup or costumes).

Suggested scenery:
A fingerpainted backdrop of a door, window and oven.
A fingerpainted backdrop of sky and greenery.

PLAY

Narrator: Let's listen to the story.
/dramatic tone/ The Gingerbread Man!

Granny is baking in the kitchen. She mimes beating the batter in the bowl with the spoon, then shaping it on the baking sheet. Then she mimes putting it in the oven.

Granny takes the baking sheet out of the oven with the oven mitts. She puts it down on the table.
Timmy and Tessa run in to say hello and give her a hug.

Granny: Hello Tessa, hello Timmy! What a nice surprise!

Tessa (pointing to the baking sheet): What's that, Granny?

Granny: A gingerbread man for you and me!
Timmy claps his hands.
Timmy: Oh, what a yummy snack!
Chorus: Oh, what a yummy snack!

Granny starts decorating the gingerbread man. As she names each part of the face, she puts the appropriate Smarties in place on the face.

Granny: Two eyes for the gingerbread man!
A nose and a mouth for the gingerbread man!

/props change quickly – we are now outdoors/
The bird mimes flying in. The real Gingerbread Man jumps up and starts running in place.

Bird (urgently): Jump, Gingerbread Man! Jump and run!

Grandpa enters and tries to catch the Gingerbread Man. The Bird urges him to escape.

Granpa: What a yummy snack!
Bird: Run, Gingerbread Man! Run!
Chorus: Run, Gingerbread Man! Run!

The Cat enters and tries to catch the Gingerbread Man. The Bird urges him to escape.

Cat: Meow! Meow! What a yummy snack!
Bird: Run, Gingerbread Man! Run!
Chorus: Run, Gingerbread Man! Run!

The Dog enters and tries to catch the Gingerbread Man. The Bird urges him to escape.

Dog: Woof! Woof! What a yummy snack!
Bird: Run, Gingerbread Man! Run!
Chorus: Run, Gingerbread Man! Run!

The Bird points to his back. The Gingerbread Man puts his arms around the Bird's waist. Grandpa, the Cat and the Dog watch them escape.

Bird: Jump, Gingerbread Man! Let's go away!
Gingerbread man: Thank you, little bird! Thank you!

Everybody join in sing the song.

Run, run, run,
Gingerbread Man, run!
Jump, jump, jump,
Gingerbread Man, jump!
Run and jump!
Run and jump!
Gingerbread Man, GO!

Then they take a bow and wave goodbye to the audience.

TESTING AND ASSESSMENT

Assessment is an integral part of the learning process and it is most successful when done through the systematic observation of pupils during the course. It cannot be seen through isolated events like exams or tests. The Unit Tests, the Formative assessment chart and End of unit assessment chart will help you in this task.

Merry Team 1 provides three types of assessment: **entry**, **summative** and **formative.**

Entry assessment is done at the beginning of the course in order to find out how much the children know in English and plan appropriate teaching strategies. Unit 0 of each level of Merry Team enables you to carry out this type of assessment.

Formative assessment is performed during the whole of the period. It is an ongoing process of gathering information on the extent of learning, on strengths and weaknesses, which the teacher can feed back into their course planning and the actual feedback they give to learners.[1]

Summative assessment is performed at the end of a specific period. It sums up attainment at the end of the course with a grade.[2]

Photocopiable assessment material (tests and charts) catering for these different types of assessment is provided in this section:

Unit Tests. Hand out a photocopy of the unit test to each pupil. Pupils complete the test individually. Once you have corrected all the tests, return them to the pupils and help them check their performance by writing the answers on the board. Make sure they file their tests in their Language Portfolio.

Formative assessment should be carried out on a daily basis using the Formative Assessment chart (p. 99). Photocopy this chart and write the pupils' names in the first column. The chart can be used to record pupils results in both oral activities (games, pair work, etc.) and written work (compositions, project work, etc.). Give each child a mark according to the marking criteria. Write any comments in the right-hand column.

Summative assessment can be performed at the end of each unit after you have marked the Unit tests. Photocopy the End of unit assessment chart (p. 100) and write the pupils' names across the top. Write the objectives of the unit you wish to evaluate and put a grade according to the assessment scale provided.

---

[1] Common European Framework of Reference for Languages: learning, teaching, assessment. 9.3.5 Formative assessment/summative assessment, p. 186.

[2] Ibid.

Tests • TEACHER'S NOTES

Test 1

1 Listen and circle.

Hand out the photocopies of the test (pp. 87-88). Explain to pupils that they have to circle the pictures according to your instructions. Repeat each sentence twice.

Script
1 Circle the pencil.
2 Circle the chair.
3 Circle Rocky.
4 Circle the book.
5 Circle the door.
6 Circle the table.

2 Count and colour.

Tell pupils to take out the following crayons: red, blue, green. Say: Show me (blue), to make sure that they all have the right crayons.
Point to the objects and ask pupils to identify them: Crayons, pencils and books. (We want to check counting in this exercise.)
Tell pupils that they are going to colour different numbers of items according to your instructions. Do the colour dictation, repeating each sentence twice. Remind them to mark the items with a dot of colour first and finish colouring when the dictation is over.

Script
1 Red. Colour three crayons red.
2 Blue. Colour two pencils blue.
3 Green. Colour one book green.

3 Label the items.

Focus attention on the words that appear in the box. Read them as pupils point to them.
The task is to label each item by copying the appropriate word on each line.

Marking instructions
Count the number of correct answers and circle the corresponding face at the bottom of the page.

Test 2

1 Listen and join.

Hand out the photocopies of the test (pp. 89-90). Point to the first exercise and read the rubric. Explain to pupils that they have to join two family members (one from each column) according to your instructions. Repeat each sentence twice.

Script
1 Join granny and grandad.
2 Join brother and sister.
3 Join dad and mum.

2 Circle the odd one out.

Point to the second exercise and read the rubric. Tell pupils that they are going to look at each row of items and circle the one that doesn't belong to the sequence. Identify the persons or items twice.

Script
1 Mum – granny – book – brother.
2 Chair – table – bed – pencil.
3 Crayon – window – book – pencil.

3 Label the persons.

Focus attention on the words that appear in the box. Read them as pupils point to them.
The task is to label each person by copying the appropriate word on each line.

Marking instructions
Count the number of correct answers and circle the corresponding face at the bottom of the page.

Test 3

1 😊 Listen and circle.

Hand out the photocopies of the test (pp. 91-92). Explain to pupils that they have to circle the pictures according to your instructions. Repeat each sentence twice.

Script

1 Circle the chicken.
2 Circle the biscuit.
3 Circle orange.
4 Circle the ice cream.
5 Circle the apple.
6 Circle the banana.

2 Count and colour.

Tell pupils to take out green, orange and yellow crayons. Say: Show me (blue), to make sure that they all have the right crayons.
Point to the objects and ask pupils to identify them: Apples, bananas, oranges. (We want to check counting in this exercise.)
Tell pupils that they are going to colour different numbers of food items according to your instructions. Do the colour dictation, repeating each sentence twice. Remind them to mark the items with a dot of colour first and finish colouring when the dictation is over.

Script

1 Green. Colour four apples green.
2 Orange. Colour three oranges orange.
3 Yellow. Colour five bananas yellow.

3 Label the items.

Focus attention on the words that appear in the box. Read them as pupils point to them.
The task is to label each item by copying the appropriate word on each line.

Marking instructions

Count the number of correct answers and circle the corresponding face at the bottom of the page.

Test 4

1 😊 Listen and circle.

Hand out the photocopies of the test (pp. 93-94). Point to the first exercise and read the rubric. Explain to pupils that they have to look at the pairs of faces and circle one according to your instructions. Repeat each sentence twice.

Script

1 He's got a big nose. Circle the big nose.
2 He's got big eyes. Circle the big eyes.
3 He's got a small mouth. Circle the small mouth.
4 He's got a big head. Circle the big head.

2 Count and circle.

Point to the second exercise and read the rubric. Pupils look at the number written next to each set and circle the appropriate number of items.

Script

1 Four crayons. Circle four crayons.
2 Five pencils. Circle five pencils.
3 Two oranges. Circle two oranges.
4 Six apples. Circle six apples.

3 Write the words.

Focus attention on the words that appear in the box. Read them as pupils point to them.
The task is to label each body part by copying the appropriate word on each line.

Marking instructions

Count the number of correct answers and circle the corresponding face at the bottom of the page.

Tests • TEACHER'S NOTE

Test 5

1 🖼 Listen and join.

Hand out the photocopies of the test (pp. 95-96).
Point to the first exercise and read the rubric. Explain to pupils that they have to join two animals (one from each column) according to your instructions. Repeat each sentence twice.

Script
1 Join the squirrel and the mouse.
2 Join the cat and the rabbit.
3 Join the bird and the fox.
4 Join the raccoon and the dog.

2 Circle the odd one out.

Point to the second exercise and read the rubric.
Tell pupils that they are going to look at each row of items and circle the one that doesn't belong to the sequence. Identify the animals and items twice.

Script
1 mouse – rabbit – granny – fox
2 raccoon – hand – bird – mouse
3 fox – cat – eight – dog

3 Label the animals.

Focus attention on the words that appear in the box.
Read them as pupils point to them.
The task is to label each animal by copying the appropriate word on each line.

Marking instructions
Count the number of correct answers and circle the corresponding face at the bottom of the page.

Test 6

1 🖼 Count and circle.

Point to the second exercise and read the rubric.
Pupils look at the number written next to each set and circle the appropriate number of items.

Script
1 Nine balls. Circle nine balls.
2 Eight sunhats. Circle eight sunhats.
3 Ten biscuits. Circle ten biscuits.

2 Find and label.

Focus attention on the words that appear in the box.
Read them as pupils point to them.
The task is to label each item by copying the appropriate word on each line.

3 🖼 Listen, read and number.

Focus attention on the scene. Tell pupils they are going to number the items from 1 to 10.
Read the text slowly, pausing after each underlined word to give them enough time to write the number.

Script
This is my <u>dad</u> and me. We're on holiday.
My dad's wearing <u>shorts</u> and <u>sandals</u>.
He's got a <u>book</u> and an <u>ice cream</u>.
I'm wearing a <u>sunhat</u>. I've got an <u>apple</u> and a <u>biscuit</u>.
My <u>cat</u> Lili is under my <u>chair</u>.

Marking instructions
Count the number of correct answers and circle the corresponding face at the bottom of the page.

Unit Test

1 Listen and circle.

(1 point each = 6 points)

2 Count and colour.

1

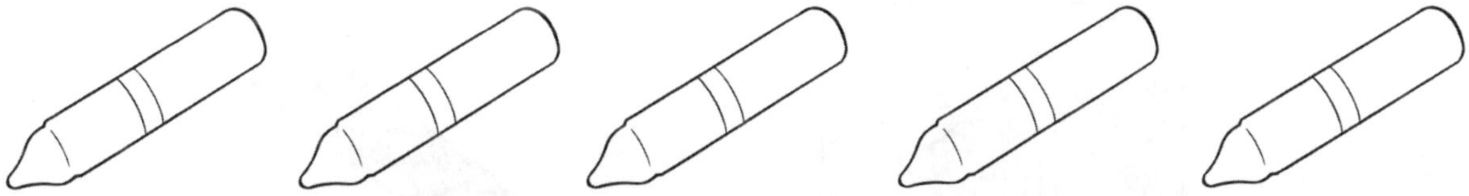

2

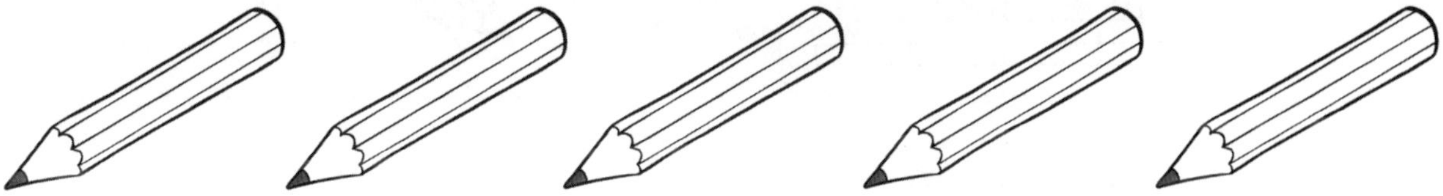

3

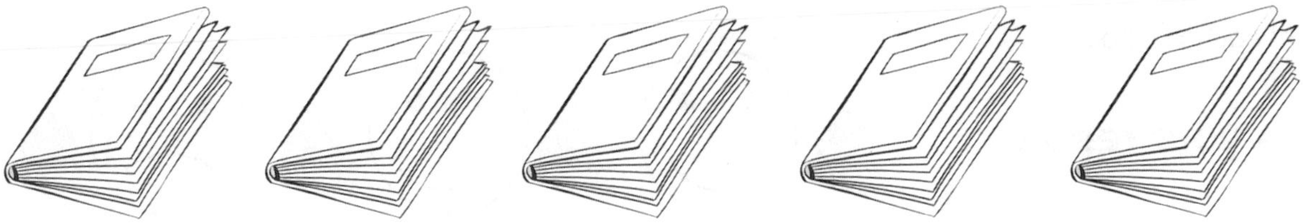

(1 point each = 3 points)

Unit Test

3 **Label the items.**

door • book • table • chair • pencil • bed • crayon • window

....

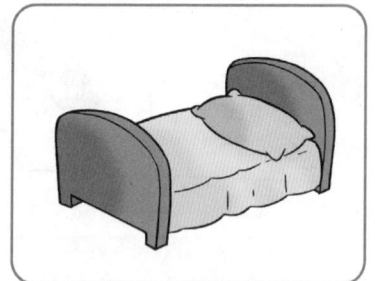

....

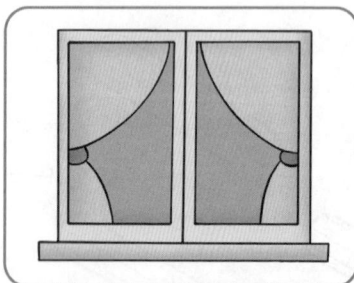

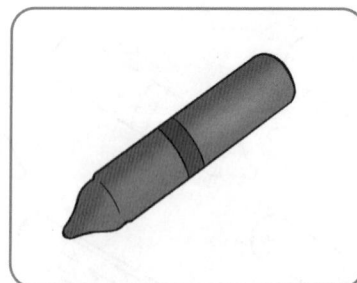

....

(1 point each = 8 points)

Circle your results.

12 – 17   **6 – 11**   **0 – 5**

Unit Test

1 😊 Listen and join.

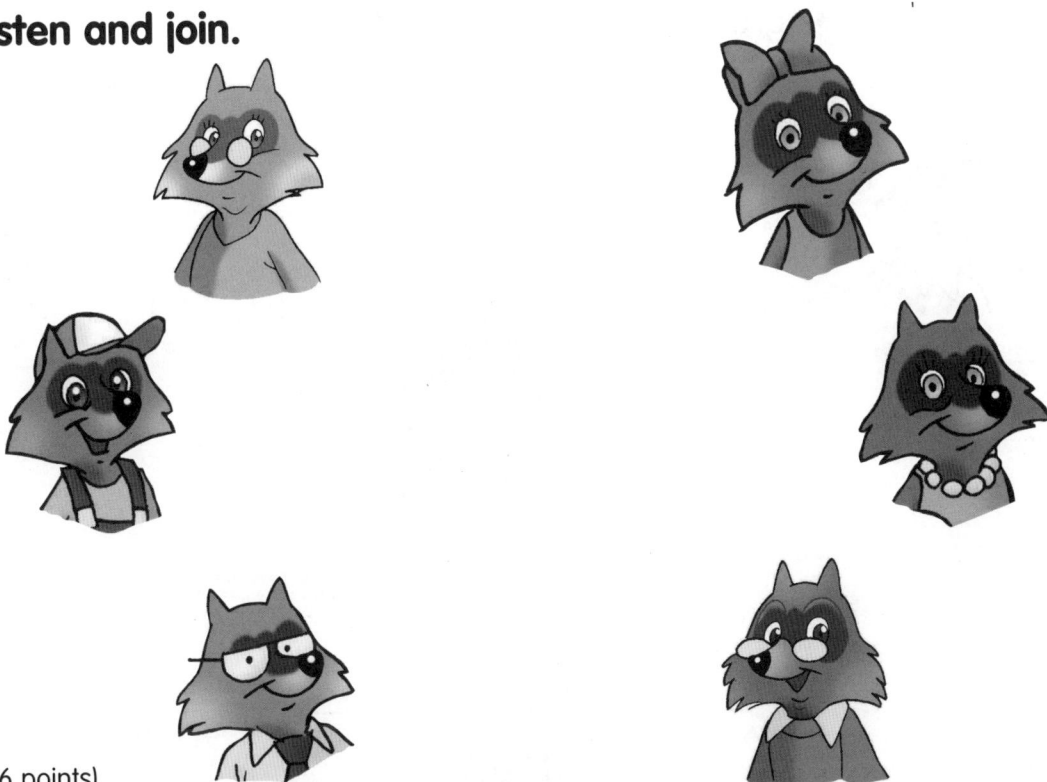

(1 point each = 6 points)

2 Circle the odd one out.

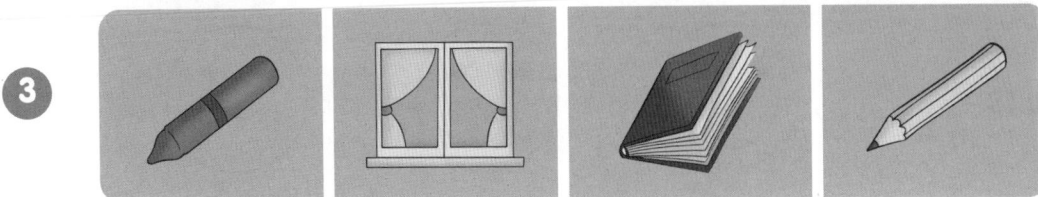

(1 point each = 3 points)

2 Unit Test

3 Label the persons.

mum • granny • sister • dad • grandad • brother

....

....

....

....

....

....

(1 point each = 6 points)

Circle your results.

11 – 15

6 - 10

0 - 5

Unit Test

1 😊 Listen and circle.

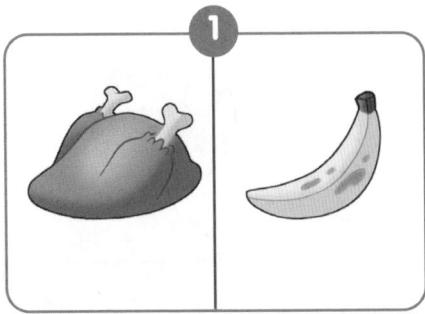

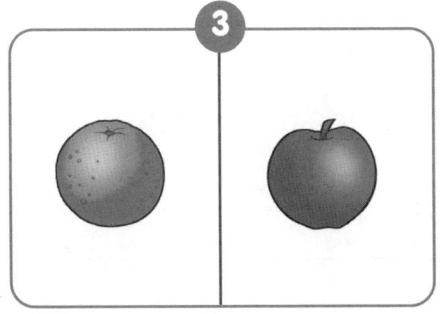

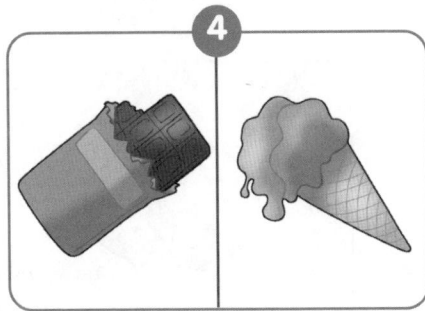

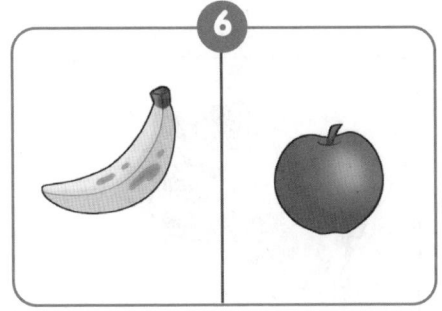

1	2	3

4	5	6

(1 point each = 6 points)

2 Count and colour.

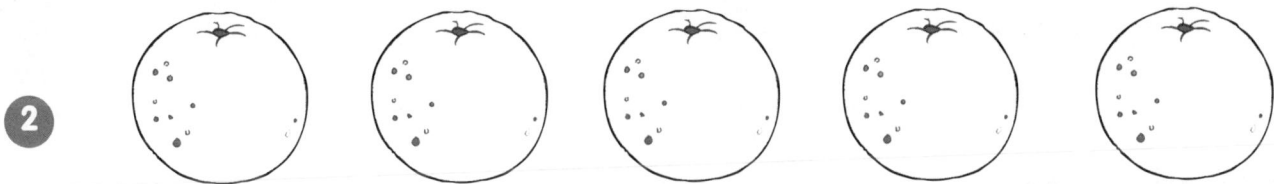

1

2

3

(1 point each = 3 points)

Unit Test

3 3 **Label the items.**

ice cream • biscuit • apple • banana • orange • chocolate • milk • chicken

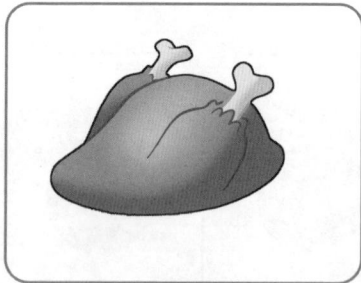

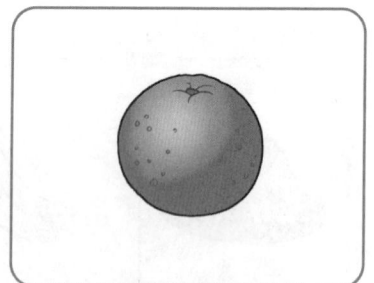

....

....

....

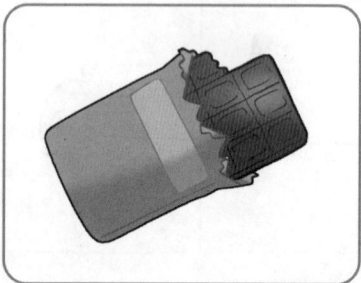

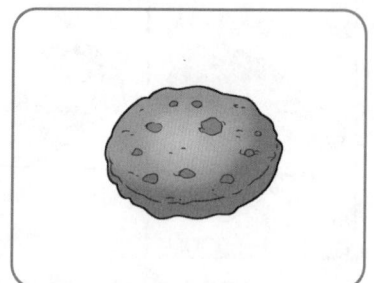

....

....

....

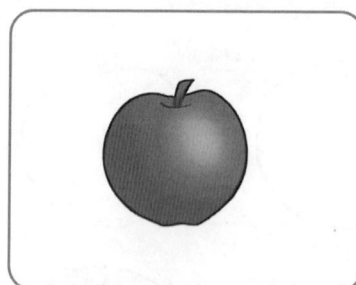

....

....

(1 point each = 8 points)

Circle your results.

12 - 17

6 - 11

0 - 5

Unit Test

1 Listen and circle.

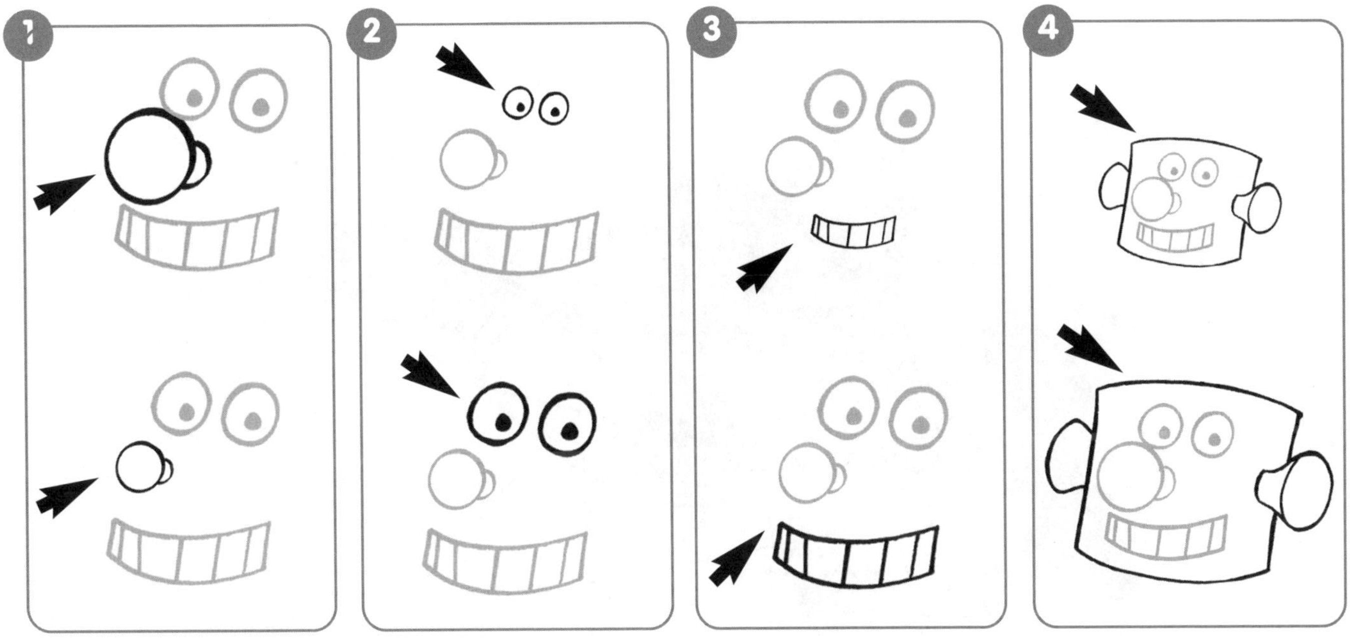

(1 point each = 4 points)

2 Count and circle.

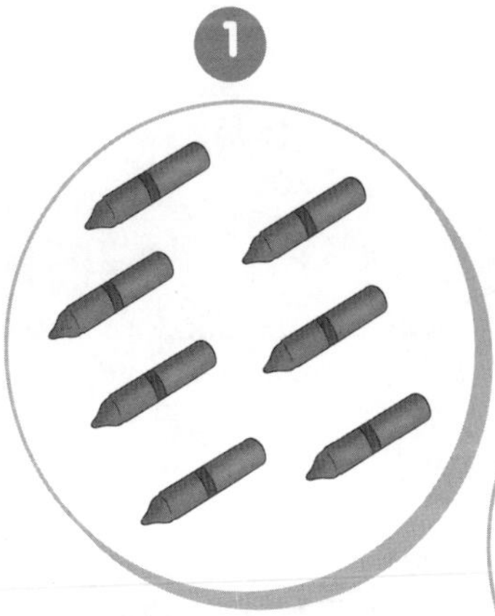

4 crayons

5 pencils

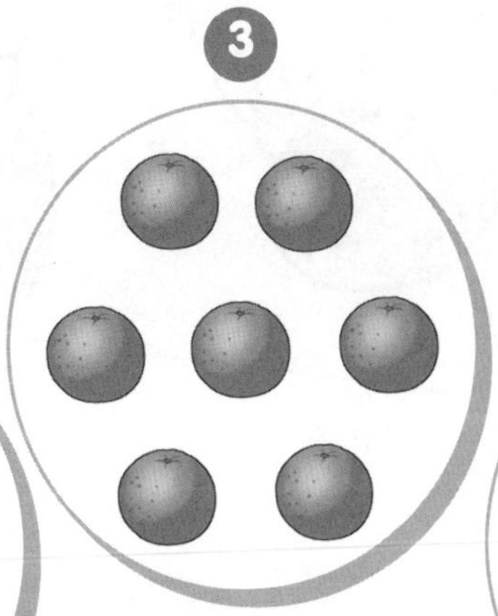

2 oranges

6 apples

(1 point each = 4 points)

Unit Test

3 **Write the words.**

legs • head • arms • eyes • feet • nose • hands • mouth

(1 point each = 8 points)

Circle your results.

10 – 16   6 – 9   0 – 5

Unit Test

1 😊 **Listen and join.**

(1 point each = 8 points)

2 **Circle the odd one out.**

1

2

3

(1 point each = 3 points)

Unit Test

3 **Label the animals.**

rabbit • dog • bird • squirrel • raccoon • mouse • cat • fox

....

....

....

....

....

....

....

....

(1 point each = 8 points)

Circle your results.

15 - 19

8 - 14

0 - 7

Unit Test

1 **Count and circle.**

1

2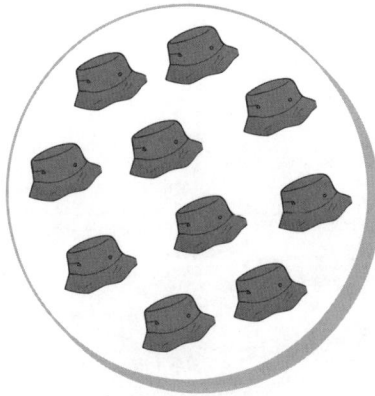

3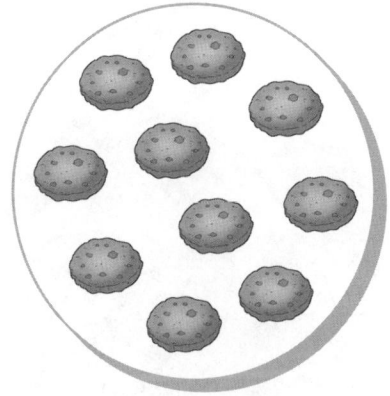

9 balls   **8 sunhats**   **10 biscuits**

(1 point each = 3 points)

2 **Find and label.**

sunglasses • shorts • ball • sandals • sunhat • rucksack

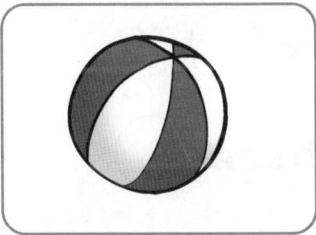

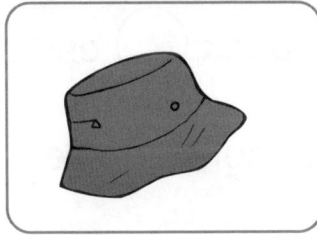

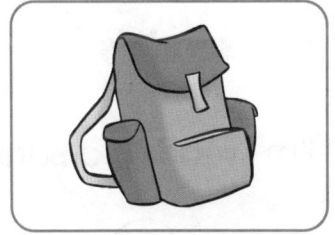

....

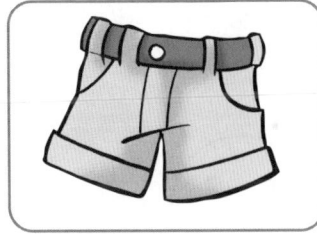

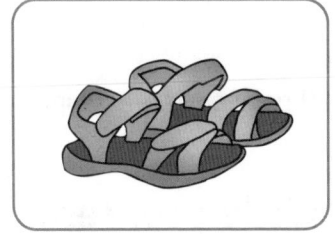

....

(1 point each = 6 points)

Unit Test

3  **Listen, read and number.**

This is my **dad** ◯ and me. We're on holiday. My dad's wearing **shorts** ◯

and **sandals** ◯ . He's got a **book** ◯ and an **ice cream** ◯ .

I'm wearing a **sunhat** ◯ . I've got an **apple** ◯ and a **biscuit** ◯ .

My **cat** ◯ Lili is under my **chair** ◯ .

(1 point each = 10 points)

Circle your results.

 **14 - 19**

 **10 - 13**

 **0 - 9**

Formative assessment

Name of activity: ....

Aim of activity: ....

Unit: .... Lesson: .... Course: ....

Pupils' names	The pupil is able to...	Marks
1		
2		
3		
4		
5		
6		
7		
8		
9		
10		
11		
12		
13		
14		
15		
16		
17		
18		
19		
20		
21		
22		
23		
24		
25		

Marking criteria: 1 excellent **2** good **3** with certain difficulties **4** with a lot of difficulties **5** not at all

End of unit assessment

Pupils' names

Unit: ....

Date: ....

Course: ....

Objectives: The pupil is able to...	1	2	3	4	5	6	7	8	9	10	11	12	13	14	15	16	17	18	19	20	21	22	23	24	25

Marking criteria: 1 excellent   2 good   3 with certain difficulties   4 with a lot of difficulties   5 not at all

Cut-out

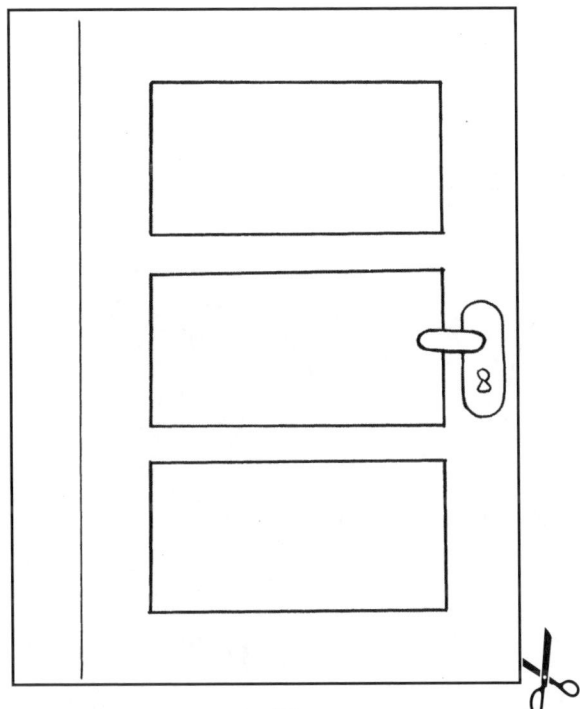

p. 7

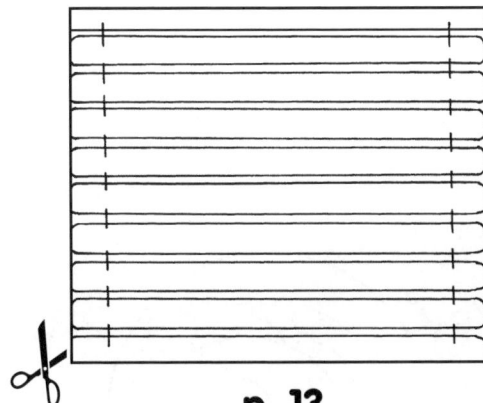

p. 13

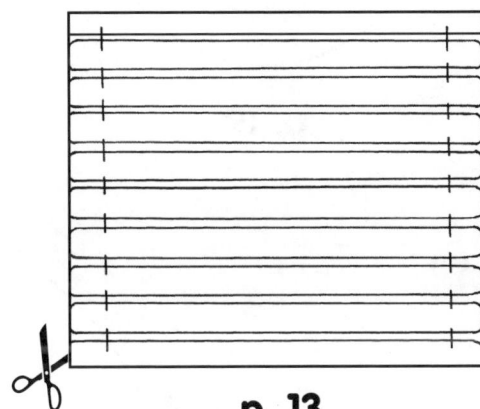

p. 13

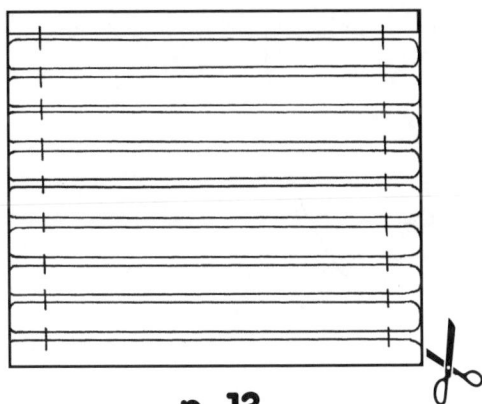

p. 13

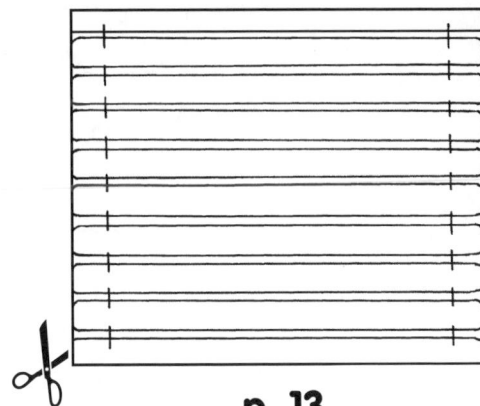

p. 13

Cut-out

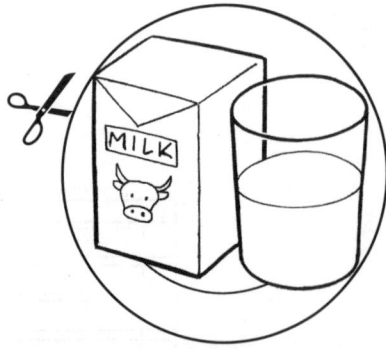

p. 19

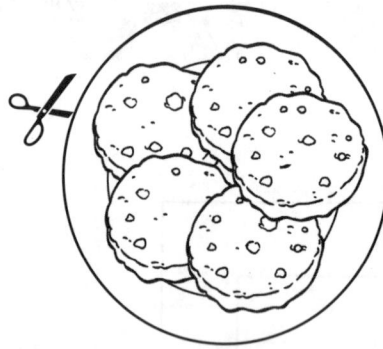

p. 19

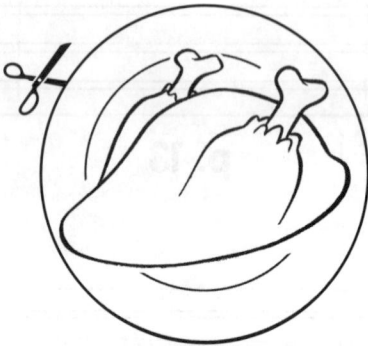

p. 19

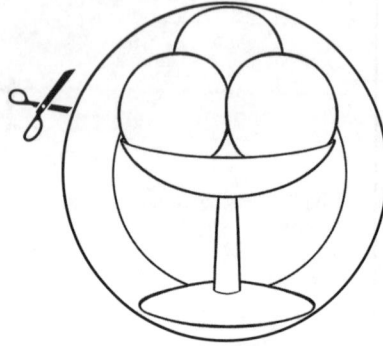

p. 19

p. 19

p. 25

Cut-out

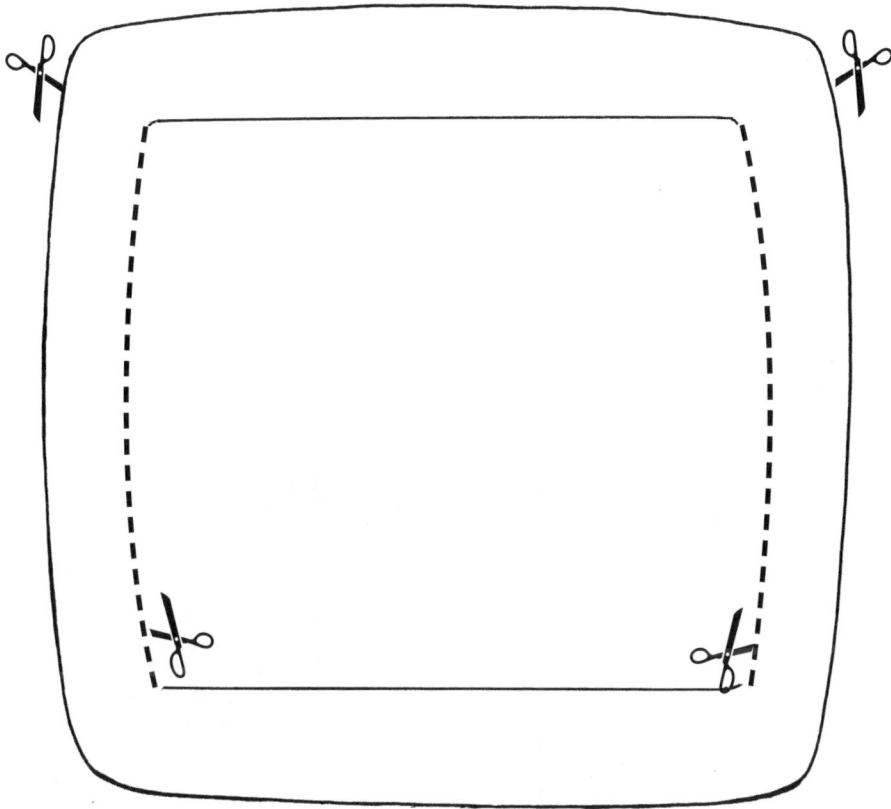

p. 31

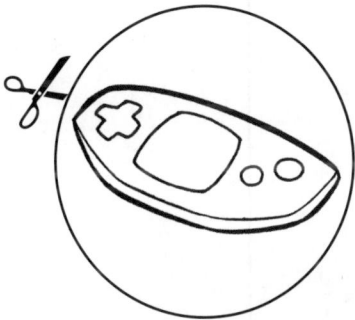

p. 37

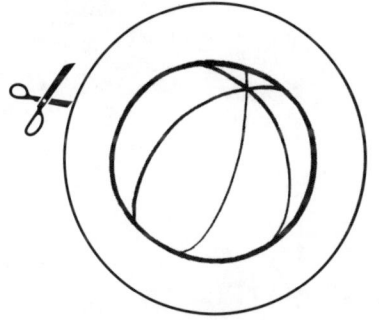

p. 37

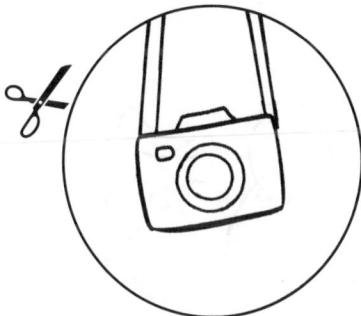

p. 37

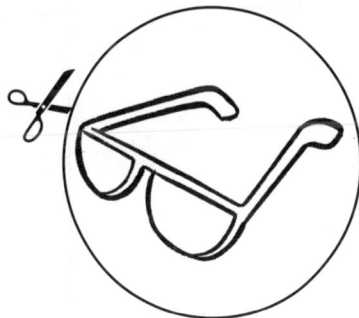

p. 37

Cut-out

p. 31